MODERN HUMORIST

PRESENTS

ONE NATION, EXTRA CHEESE

Your Guide to the Bestest Country Ever!

THREE RIVERS PRESS • NEW YORK

Published by Three Rivers Press, New York, New York.
Member of the Crown Publishing Group,
a division of Random House, Inc.
www.randomhouse.com

Three Rivers Press and the Tugboat design are registered trade-marks of Random House, Inc.

Printed in the United States of America

Design by Patrick Broderick/Modern Humorist

Library of Congress Cataloging-in-Publication Data is available upon request.

ISBN 0-609-80979-2

10 9 8 7 6 5 4 3 2 1

First Edition

MODERN HUMORIST

PRESENTS

ONE NATION, EXTRA CHEESE

Your Guide to the Bestest Country Ever!

Written by
John Aboud, Patrick Broderick,
Michael Colton, and Martha Keavney

Designed by Patrick Broderick

Concept created by Patrick Broderick

Additional material by Paul Bacon, Nick Danforth, Brian Dermody,
Charlie Grandy, Josh Greenman, Francis Heaney, Lauren Kirchner, Karen Lurie,
Phil Maciak, Matt Murray, Nick Nadel, Neil Pasricha, Daniel Radosh,
Alexandra Ringe, Beth Sherman, Seaton Smith, Daniel Tobey, Noam Weinstein

State quarters by Robert Nassau

Thanks to Kate Barker, Diane Bullock, Rebecca Clement, Nic Duquette,
Pete Fornatale, Louis Giliberti, Tim Roethgen, Kim Witherspoon

Modern Humorist Founders
John Aboud and Michael Colton

ABOUT THE AUTHOR

Modern Humorist, an entertainment company based in
Brooklyn, produces an award-winning comedy magazine
at www.ModernHumorist.com. Modern Humorist's
previous books include *Rough Draft: Pop Culture the
Way It Almost Was* and *My First Presidentiary: A Scrapbook
by George W. Bush*.

Modern Humorist material appears regularly in magazines
(including *TV Guide*, *Fortune*, and *New York*) and on
National Public Radio. The company also operates an
ad-services division, Humor Dynamics
(www.HumorDynamics.com), which has developed
campaigns for Microsoft and Time Warner Cable, among
others. Modern Humorist has developed a pilot for
television and produced a live comedy show in
Manhattan.

To give your feedback about this book, or to find out
more about Modern Humorist, send a message to
feedback@modernhumorist.com. Additional information
is available at www.ModernHumorist.com/onenation.
Sign up for Banter, Modern Humorist's weekly newsletter,
at www.ModernHumorist.com/house/banter.

CONTENTS

INTRODUCTION

WELCOME TO AMERICA

You might not be looking for the promised land,
but you might find it anyway (hunnh!)

—James Brown, "Living in America"

This hymn to the beauty of America attempts to describe the grandeur of its vast and varied regions, but America's majesty can't easily be summed up in mere words, even funky ones. We'll let the pictures do the talking.

THE UNITED STATES is often referred to as a "melting pot" in that it boils away the character of immigrants from many diverse backgrounds and nationalities. That's right, America's ancestors were foreigners, just like you and me! Foreign men and women came by ship to America—many against their will—and built this country's mighty railroads, gleaming shopping malls and state-of-the-art prison facilities. Today, millions of travelers come to America every year to experience its culture first-hand, as well as to purchase blue jeans and view movies that won't be released in their home countries for another two weeks.

The global perception of American culture is shaped by popular television exports like "Nash Bridges" and "Diagnosis: Murder." Accurate as these programs are, first-time visitors often find themselves confused by the strange customs practiced by Americans. To the uninitiated, America can seem larger than life, despite its actually being at ¾ scale. Many visitors expect a place where savage gunfighters run free, everything is for sale and nobody can be trusted. Of course, these notions are exaggerations. Gunfights are confined to nightclubs and public playgrounds, and many things are emphatically not for sale, like Vegemite, David Hasselhoff albums, over-the-counter Percodan and a halfway decent brioche.

Perception   **Reality**

This book will unlock the secrets to finding and enjoying the myriad charms of this beautiful and unique country where the only rule is "Expect the unexpected!" That, plus "No smoking in public spaces," "Don't carry an open container of alcohol (except in New Orleans)" and some others.

American Citizens

Who lives in America? A peek at the most recent census gives us a clue:

Total number of Americans: 138,053,563*

*including "fe-males": 281,421,906

Number of Americans who asked not to be counted due to low self-esteem: 76,502

Percentage who included at least one gun when counting their children: 64%

Race:

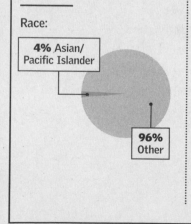

4% Asian/Pacific Islander

96% Other

Number who doodled on the form: 124,094,597

Number whose doodles involved a personified Census form stabbing a personified America with a pencil: 58,163,492

Most popular profession: Middle manager

Most popular overall: Alicia Hunter, Baton Rouge, LA

Biggest fear:

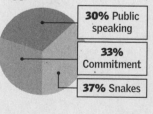

30% Public speaking

33% Commitment

37% Snakes

Ethnic Diversity

Because of the great number of immigrants living in the United States, you're likely to see people of many different nationalities and ethnic backgrounds during your visit. Unless, of course, your visit is to Minnesota (see page 32). This volatile mix of races, colors and creeds means that American corporations have become very sensitive to the importance of workplace diversity. To this end, the all-male, all-Caucasian staffs of most Fortune 500 companies take pains to use stock photography of ethnic- and gender-balanced groups when putting together commercials and other advertisements.

Another interesting by-product of this ethnic mix is that a number of foreign words and phrases have made their way into spoken American English. See if there are any you recognize!

"Ciao!" = "See you later!"

"Sayonara!" = "See you later!"

"Bon voyage!" = "See you later!"

"Hasta la vista, baby!" = "I am about to shoot you."

THE UPPER RIGHT

The upper-right portion of America is a study in contrasts: Sprawling urban hellholes interrupt huge swaths of rural backwater. Humid, sweltering summers give way to bone-chilling winters. And of course, this part of the country is host to one of the bitterest rivalries in all of women's professional football—the WPFL's Syracuse Sting vs. the New England Storm. Despite the dichotomous nature of the region, the people of the Northeast all share one personality: unpleasant.

New England

MASSACHUSETTS is renowned for its many institutions of higher learning. While crosstown rival Harvard University has undertaken the responsibility of educating most of America's sitcom writers, many of today's greatest technological achievements have originated from the Massachusetts Institute of Technology (MIT).

Early planning of the Internet at MIT, 1961

MAINE, the northernmost state of the continental United States, was an early proponent of the temperance movement of the 1800s. Continuing this New England tradition of safety at the expense of fun, Maine's biggest attractions today are lighthouses and covered bridges.

RHODE ISLAND is the smallest state in America. If you were to get every citizen of Rhode Island to lie in a straight line end to end, it would be much more trouble than it's worth.

New York

NEW YORK CITY is arguably the most recognizable place in America—most of the world's crime dramas originate here, as do many of the world's criminals. Most people are familiar with New York through television shows like "Seinfeld" and "Sex and the City," but neurotic Jews and slutty socialites make up only a fraction of the city's residents.

Perception: Neurotic Jews and slutty socialites

Reality: This guy

HOMELESS WILL BOTHER YOU FOR FOOD

You can't think of New York City without thinking of its most illustrious mayor, Rudy Giuliani. Though beloved for his sensitive response to the city's tragedies, his tough anti-crime, anti-art policies made him something of a controversial figure during his tenure as mayor.

FUN FACT

Besides maple syrup and hippies, **VERMONT**'s best-loved export is Ben & Jerry's ice cream. This dessert is hugely popular with American marijuana enthusiasts afflicted with the "munchies," as it provides an alternative to purchasing ice cream, candy, cookies, pretzels and other snack foods separately— Ben & Jerry combine them all into a delicious frozen medley.

New York City's crime rate has decreased drastically from its 1980s zenith. Even so, visitors to the Big Apple should still keep a watchful eye on their belongings. Pickpockets still exist, and can be lurking in unexpected spots.

An open handbag can be an easy target for pickpockets

Keep your wallet in a front pocket to discourage thieves

Keep expensive cameras out of sight when not in use

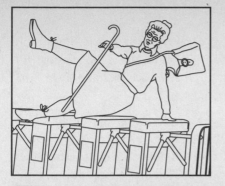

To ride the subway, you could purchase a token, but this will brand you as a tourist, making you an easy mark for pickpockets. Instead, do as the locals do and jump the turnstile.

There are many New York attractions outside of Manhattan. A favorite upstate New York tourist spot is

NIAGARA FALLS, a majestic natural waterfall on the Canadian border. Several attempts have been made to ride down the waterfall in makeshift barrels, kayaks, and even a Jet Ski™. Nearly all have been fatal, but don't let that stop you.

Niagara Falls

New Jersey

New Jersey has long been unfairly referred to as "the armpit of America." In truth, it's more like the ribcage of America—nice enough, but easy to overlook in favor of the sexy bits to the north.

Unbeknownst to many, New Jersey is full of beautiful scenery year-round. New Jerseyites look forward to the fall, when they can observe the autumnal arrival of lush shades of gold, chestnut and brown. Of course we're talking about the lavish coif of local rock musician Jon Bon Jovi.

Premier gaming destination **ATLANTIC CITY** is the Vegas of the East, minus the gay tiger wranglers and the side trip to the Moonlite Bunnyranch. Tourists looking for legalized prostitution in Atlantic City are encouraged to date Donald Trump.

Pennsylvania

Pennsylvania is where you'll find the **HERSHEY CHOCOLATE FACTORY,** as well as the home of America's second-favorite waxy treats, the **CRAYOLA CRAYON FACTORY**. Both facilities offer public tours, which are a great way to get children excited about a future in monotonous assembly-line work.

PHILADELPHIA is a favorite of both art and history buffs, as it houses not only the Liberty Bell and Rodin's "The Thinker," but also the famous sculpture of Sylvester Stallone from "Rocky III."

Art lovers in Philadelphia

Washington, D.C.

Washington, D.C., is the nation's capital, nerve center of the United States government. You have probably seen Washington on the American television program "The West Wing," or in one of the many other historic televised events that have used the District of Columbia as a backdrop.

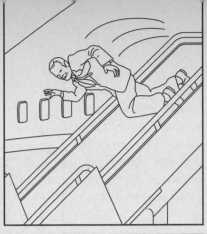

FROM TOP TO BOTTOM:
Gerald Ford,
Air Force One, 1976;
Marion Barry,
Vista Hotel, 1990;
Really not that big
a deal after all, 1993

Washington, D.C., is also home to the Smithsonian Institution, the world's largest conglomeration of museums. Scholars come from around the world to see the important artifacts in the Smithsonian's collection.

JACKET WORN BY HENRY WINKLER ON "HAPPY DAYS" TV PROGRAM

CAPTAIN JAMES T. KIRK'S "PHASER" PROP FROM "STAR TREK" TELEVISION PROGRAM

FROM TOP TO BOTTOM: Fonzie's jacket from "Happy Days"; Kirk's phaser from "Star Trek"; former Massachusetts governor and presidential candidate Michael Dukakis

FORMER MASSACHUSETTS GOVERNOR MICHAEL DUKAKIS

Maryland

Maryland's best-known city is probably **BALTIMORE,** sometimes jokingly called "Charm City." Visitors from abroad are often puzzled about merchandise boldly emblazoned with the word "HOMICIDE." No, it's not that Baltimoreans are proud of their manslaughter rate—"Homicide" is the name of a long-ago canceled Baltimore-based television

program. While such a program may seem an odd choice for a city to embrace, there are no other appropriate Baltimore-based productions.

Actor Divine in the Baltimore-set romp "Pink Flamingos"

U.S. REGIONS

TOURIST BOARD SLOGANS

Alabama: "Civil rights for nearly 35 years!"

Arizona: "The humping isn't all that's dry out here."

California: "Ain't no party like a West Coast party, 'cause a West Coast party don't stop."

Delaware: "The thinking man's Maryland!"

Hawaii: "Where the age of consent is fourteen."

Louisiana: "Take a chance on our murder rate."

Maine: "Home of President George Bush. The wimp, not the dumb one."

Maryland: "Doesn't it feel good to Payless?"

Massachusetts: "Can you smell what Plymouth Rock is cookin'?"

Michigan: "Now in two parts for your comfort and convenience."

Missouri: "I bet you've never seen an arch <u>this</u> big before!"

Nevada: "$15 cover, 2 drink minimum."

Oregon: "A little slice of Canada."

Rhode Island: "Existence is but a futile arrangement with death."

Tennessee: "As mentioned in the Arrested Development song."

Texas: "A great place to be old and white."

Utah: "A great place to be white and fanatic."

THE LEFT SIDE

The stereotype of the left side of America is one of sunny beachfront property peopled with grizzled hippies and out-of-work actors who spend all day racing down the highway in their gas-guzzling convertible sports cars while snorting lines of cocaine off the flat, tan stomachs of their teenage mistresses. In reality, sports cars are actually very fuel-efficient.

The Pacific Northwest

The Pacific Northwest is home to gloom and rain year-round, making it a popular destination for depressed drug addicts. It's no surprise that **SEATTLE'S** most famous landmark is a needle! Besides heroin abuse, other popular Northwest exports are flannel shirts, three-dollar coffee and Microsoft Office.

Famous Northwesterners include Microsoft founder and celebrity litigant Bill Gates, sexy elderly actress Dyan Cannon and psychedelic musician Jimi Hendrix, who became a symbol of hometown pride in his native Seattle by leaving the country to become successful and die of a barbiturate overdose.

Hendrix inspired the construction of a Seattle museum called the Experience Music Project. An amorphous blob dedicated to the greatness of defunct '60s and '70s rock acts, the EMP is essentially a brick-and-mortar version of *Rolling Stone* publisher Jann Wenner.

California

Down the coast is sunny California. Southern California is home to orange groves, Disneyland, Hell's Angels and golden brown skies. Northern California is home to people who hate Southern California.

The television and motion picture industries are based in California because of the state's breathtaking natural scenery and supply of computer nerds who can erase that scenery in post-production. Most of the popular entertainment enjoyed around the world was filmed in the Golden State—watch closely and you'll see plenty of the state's attractions.

TOP: Golden Gate Bridge ("Dirty Harry");
MIDDLE: Disneyland ("Lethal Weapon");
BOTTOM: Beverly Hills ("The Beverly Hillbillies")

Nevada

Unlike its neighboring states, Nevada doesn't prosecute vice crimes—it profits from them! Nevadans enjoy legal gambling, and visitors are often shocked at the variety and placement of slot machines.

Nevada is also famous for its prostitutes. Yes, legal brothels exist in the Silver State, but don't worry, they're thoroughly modern—not the seedy Victorian-era bawdy houses you might imagine.

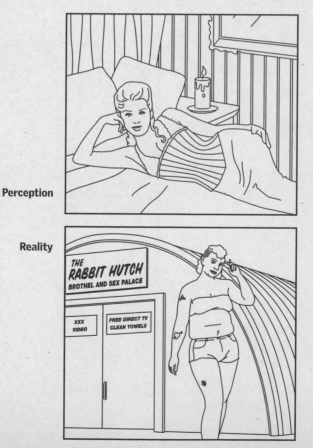

Perception

Reality

THE
RABBIT HUTCH
BROTHEL AND SEX PALACE

XXX
VIDEO

FREE DIRECT TV
CLEAN TOWELS

The Bumpy States

In the rugged country and wide-open spaces of the Central Northwestern states, it's important to the residents to maintain warm human relationships. You'll notice many social clubs, organizations and even fortified compounds where people of like interests can get together. Stop by any of these places and ask for a tour—they'll be happy to answer your questions.

Idaho

Montana

Colorado

The Southwest

The Southwestern United States is mostly arid desert dotted with cactuses, privately owned golf courses and cool cow skulls. In fact, the Southwest offers a plethora of unusual animal souvenirs, from scorpion bolo ties to rattlesnake bolo ties to beautiful photographic prints of the local fauna.

Don't be fooled: The "jackalope" is a vicious predator.

UTAH is home to some of the best ski resorts in the country as well as some spectacular scenery. People come from near and far to marvel at the weathered canyons and craggy ranges of resident Robert Redford's aging face. His Sundance Institute sponsors an independent film festival in Park City every year, and if you like pretending you're interested in independent film it's a festival you won't want to miss.

FUN FACT

?

DID YOU KNOW...?

The origin of the name "Oregon" is unknown and is probably a pretty boring story.

NEW MEXICO attracts visitors not only from outside America but from outside the solar system! Roswell, New Mexico, is rumored to be the site of a secret government facility where a UFO crashed decades ago. Don't worry—the only aliens here now are the illegal ones bussing your table.

Roswell

DON'T MISS Devils Tower, a spectacular natural rock formation in Wyoming. Does the flat-topped tower look familiar to you? It may be because you've seen it in the film "Close Encounters of the Third Kind." Or it may be déjà vu (French, "already seen"), the illusory phenomenon of feeling that you remember events and experiences when encountering them for the first time.

DON'T MISS taking a mule ride down into the Grand Canyon. But remember, mules are sterile hybrids and cannot reproduce. Don't embarrass yourself by asking for mule sperm as a souvenir.

AVOID a certain mule named "Pepito" at Canyon Expeditions, Grand Canyon National Park.

THE BOTTOM

From the steamy bayous of the Mississippi River delta to the sun-drenched plains of the Texas Panhandle to the sizzling nightclubs of Miami Beach, the southern part of America harbors the perfect warm, moist breeding grounds for many disease-carrying mosquitoes and parasites. The area is also home to a plethora of unique cultures, each with its own zesty music, tangy cuisine and incomprehensible accent.

The unifying characteristic of the South is the sense of history you will find there. Southerners retain a living memory of that historic conflict which almost tore the nation asunder so many years ago: the 1996 World Series.

The Deep South

Your conception of America's Deep South has probably been formed by movie and television portrayals of dirt-poor sharecroppers, redneck sheriffs, half-mad Bible-thumping preachers and mysterious caddies who can help troubled young golfers regain their "authentic swing." In fact, Dixie, once plagued with rural poverty and illiteracy, has changed dramatically into a dynamic center of industry. You might say the Deep South has gone through an evolution, were the concept of evolution not blasphemous heresy.

Did you know that "rock and roll"—a genre you may be familiar with through bands like The Cardigans and Soft Cell—originated in America? Tour **MEMPHIS, TENNESSEE,** where the Delta Blues evolved into a revolutionary sound and an entirely new way to cheat African-Americans out of their royalties.

And of course you'll want to make a pilgrimage to **GRACELAND,** where Elvis Presley spent his last years shooting TV sets, popping prescription drugs, gorging on fried peanut butter and banana sandwiches and living out other aspects of the American Dream.

Florida

Florida is best-known as the temporary home of Elián Gonzalez and the birthplace of the notorious butterfly ballot, which confused elderly voters in **PALM BEACH COUNTY.**

The "Butterfly Ballot"

However, Palm Beach, the graphic design capital of the world, has long been known for bewildering imagery.

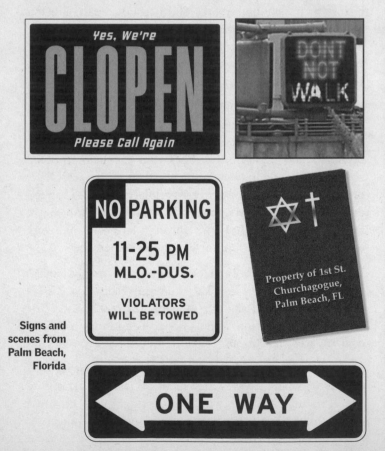

Signs and scenes from Palm Beach, Florida

Texas

The denizens of the Lone Star State proudly proclaim that everything is bigger in Texas, and they're right: From their buttocks to their hairdos to the percentage of Death Row inmates whose lawyers slept through their trial, Texas is larger. You'll find a proportional pride of place among native Texans, who wear T-shirts with slogans like "American by birth, Texan by the Grace of God." There isn't room on the shirt to mention being a citizen of our global community, but the sentiment is there.

Cowboys still exist in Texas and in the novels of Larry McMurtry, but their way of life has changed—the pickup truck has replaced the horse, and some have left the ranches altogether to work in the entertainment industry.

Modern cowboy

New Orleans

In this lively Creole city, feast on delicious seafood gumbo or stroll the historic French Quarter munching beignets. Hear authentic zydeco and cast a "voodoo" spell on your enemies. Cling to a delusional world of genteel refinement until Stanley Kowalski, played by a young Marlon Brando, brutally shatters your illusions and your sanity.

TRAVEL TIPS

DON'T MISS Colonial Williamsburg in Virginia, where actors in period costume guide you through typical Colonial scenes. You'll be surprised to find that the 18th-century colonists spent most of their time explaining wig-making to each other, over and over, all day long.

AVOID state highway speed traps. Locals are usually left alone, so try to pass for a native by driving an orange Dodge Charger and referring to it as the "General Lee." If you are followed by a police car, jump over creeks and say things like "That'll make him madder'n a long-haired dog in a tub of fleas."

The street parties of Mardi Gras in New Orleans combine the esoteric traditions of an 18th-century French Catholic festival with the class and elegance of a "Girls Gone Wild" video. During Mardi Gras anything goes, and when we say "anything," we mean partial nudity. Be sure to bring plenty of plastic beads, which can be used as currency to obtain glimpses of female breasts. The world-famous Pat O'Brien's Bayou Hurricane Bahama Mama Colada Shooter, however, will set you back nine bucks.

FUN FACT

DID YOU KNOW...?

The state disease of Arkansas is rickets, and not chlamydia as widely believed.

MINNESOTA

Let's take a look at a typical Midwestern state to get an idea of what life is like in the heartland.

Dotted with crystal-clear lakes, gently rolling hills and doughy, gullible descendants of Scandinavian settlers, Minnesota's landscape is enhanced by its thousands of megamalls and the spacious parking lots next to them. The noble buffalo who once freely roamed the plains are long gone, but the proud Ojibway and Sioux who hunted them are thriving, thanks to Americans' love of loose slots.

LEFT: Minnesota state flag. Each state has its own flag, filled with cryptic symbolism and non-English text.

RIGHT: Minnesota's population is centered around the "Twin Cities" of Minneapolis and St. Paul. The remainder of the state is mostly uninhabitable wasteland.

The Mall of America

Perhaps the most popular Minnesota attraction is the Mall of America. The Mall is like a city within a city—resources include a wedding chapel, an infirmary, a fully accredited technical college and a bankruptcy court (not to mention the famous indoor rollercoaster, which features two loops and a stopover at The Sharper Image). Spending a day at the Mall of America is like spending a year locked inside a smaller mall.

The Mall of America features many one-of-a-kind Minnesota stores and restaurants (Abercrombie and Fitch, Lady Foot Locker, Orange Julius, and Sam Goody, to name a few). To find a similar shopping experience, you would have to drive several miles to another mall.

FUN FACT

DID YOU KNOW...?

Henry Wadsworth Longfellow poem "The Song of Hiawatha" is set in Minnesota. Most people can recite the first line "By the shore of Gitche Gumee..." but don't know that the poem is about a bumbling Indian who tries to catch a smart-alecky rabbit.

Regional Delicacies

At outdoor festivals you will find vendors selling delicious dishes like walleye fish broiled in butter and served on a stick, "corndogs" on a stick, chicken on a stick and pizza on a stick. If you get tired of eating food from a stick, here are four words for you: deep fried cheese curds! (Minnesota technicians are developing ways to serve this specialty on a stick, but for now, it's stick-free.) For dessert, kids will love ice cream pressed into the shape of Pikachu's head, dipped in chocolate and mounted on a stick. At fairs and carnivals, air-puffed colored sugar ("cotton candy") on a stick is quite popular and delightfully inedible.

Sightseeing

A popular Minnesota attraction is the **PILLSBURY FACTORY** tour, where you can watch as greasy dough is squirted into cardboard tubes, which are then sold as ready-to-heat rolls, muffins and other bread-like objects. Visitors to the central offices of Pillsbury are always asking to meet the company's lovable "Doughboy." Unfortunately, security guard Tom O'Brien succumbed to complications from obesity last year.

Entertainment

Minnesota is home to a lively music scene. Minnesotan Bob Dylan gained fame by changing his name and leaving town, but one of the state's most famous musicians still owns lavender real estate here. **PAISLEY PARK,** Prince's famous recording studio, has undergone as many name changes as its owner, including "Fuchsia Grove," "Where I Keep Apollonia" and "The Building Formerly Known as General Mills Processing and Refinement Plant #4."

No study of Minnesota would be complete without a mention of its most famous elected official, a colorful raconteur whose checkered past includes a pro-wrestling career and the wearing of women's clothing! Yes, of course we're talking about Minnesota State Auditor Judith H. Dutcher.

TRAVEL TIPS

DON'T MISS the Minnesota Renaissance Festival, weekends in August and September. Truly art thou a churlish varlet if thou misseth this. Hie thee to yon goodly faire off Highway 169 a few miles south of Shakopee.

DON'T MISS the Paul Bunyan Family Fun Amusement Park in the Brainerd area. There's nothing kids like better than a mythical giant in a flannel shirt.

VISITOR INFORMATION

When to Visit

While there's never a bad time to visit the United States, various localities do have periods of inclement weather that can hamper sightseeing and respiration. To avoid disappointment, call your destination ahead of time and ask if they expect adverse weather or unpredictable natural disasters during your stay.

Sorry!
Seattle is closed due to rain. Come back soon!

America is often quite warm, thanks to pollution. Americans have been instrumental in ridding the world of the "ozone layer," a thick cloud of poisonous gases that blocks the earth's clear view of the sun. As a result, America has enjoyed a much warmer climate than in years past.

Sioux Falls, South Dakota, Dec. 1975

Sioux Falls, South Dakota, Dec. 2001

During the summer season, it's a good idea to shield yourself from the sun's deadly rays. Protect your skin with a high-SPF sunscreen (ask any passerby to help you apply it) and a wide-brimmed hat. If you're fair-skinned, you'll want to wear an outfit that provides more coverage.

Inadequate protection

Adequate protection

What to Bring

Almost anything you might need can be purchased in America, with some exceptions (see "Drugs and Alcohol," page 87). The one thing you must bring with you is a valid passport. Remember, America is not one of the "backwater" countries where a bribe to a customs official will get you across the border with no questions asked—the graft in America takes place at a much higher level and often requires a trained lobbyist.

Some forms of photo identification can be purchased in America, but not all of them are accepted as legal identification. Only a handful of states recognize the "Official Bikini Inspector Card."

Some visitors, concerned about the safety of American drinking water, bring water filtration systems or purification tablets with them. This is unnecessary. American water is chemically treated with the same germ-killing chlorine used in public swimming pools, meaning it's perfectly safe to drink. Should you get any in your eyes, however, you'll want to flush them immediately with imported bottled water, or any other sealed beverage.

Flush your eyes immediately

Strong, sturdy clothing is always a good idea. Many visitors to America purchase denim or canvas "cargo pants," which are durable, comfortable and provide a number of pockets in which to store cameras, money, gum and other, smaller pairs of pants.

RIGHT: Cargo pants provide ample storage space

CURRENCY

American paper currency recently underwent a redesign—the drab "greenbacks" of old have been replaced with drab computerized bills. Decades in the making, these bills have such intricate artwork that counterfeiters would need access to some sort of "digital scanner" or "color Xerox machine" to duplicate them. Still, it's a good idea to familiarize yourself with American money to avoid being swindled. Can you guess which of these is not real U.S. money?

1 U.S. currency
2 Probably U.S. currency
3 Not U.S. currency
4 Valid currency only in New York City
5 Not U.S. currency

Credit Cards

You can also, of course, use credit cards in America. They are accepted almost everywhere, even for transactions that you might expect to be on a cash-only system (see "Drugs and Alcohol," page 87, and "Dating and Sex," page 117). If you don't already have a credit card, you should consider getting one so that you can live as Americans do—beyond their means and drowning in a whirlpool of longing and self-recrimination.

How to Use an ATM Machine

In the United States, banks have all but eliminated human tellers in favor of money-vending devices known as ATM machines (short for Automated Teller Machine machines). What these mechanical cashiers lack in charisma, friendliness and sympathy, they more than make up for in exorbitant fees.

To use an Automated Teller Machine machine, you must punch in your PIN number (Personal Identification Number number). With the money you withdraw, you can take the SAT test, travel to OPEC countries, operate an IBM machine with an LCD display on a LAN network, or buy an ABM missile and aim it at a DMZ zone so you can later watch it on the CNN news network. But watch out for the HIV virus!

Due to a surplus of copper and nickel, the United States Mint recently introduced quarters representing every state in the country. You may encounter some in your travels, including these rarities:

NORTH CAROLINA
1788
BILLY AND BENNY McCRUI
WORLD'S HEAVIEST TWINS
b. 1946,
HENDERSONVILLE
2000
E PLURIBUS UNUM

COLORADO
1855
THE RECTANGULAR STATE
2000
E PLURIBUS UNUM

VERMONT
1791
THE PLACE WHERE JIM FEENEY LOST HIS VIRGINITY
MAY 24, 1955
2000
E PLURIBUS UNUM

HAWAII
1959
MAGNUM, P.I.
2000
E PLURIBUS UNUM

WASHINGTON, D.C.
1790

BITCH SET
ME UP

2000

FLORIDA
1841

THE
BUTTERFLY
BALLOT

2000

E PLURIBUS UNUM

MARYLAND
1788

HEAVY
METAL
PARKING
LOT

JUDAS PRIEST
CAPITOL CENTER, LANDOVER

2000

E PLURIBUS UNUM

MEXICO
2001

Rightfully
Ours

2000

E PLURIBUS UNUM

ACCOMMODATIONS

America offers an abundance of lodging choices for the weary traveler, from deluxe luxury suites to park benches with some newspaper.

Budget Lodging

American motor hotels, or "motels," are small, reasonably priced lodgings that house motoring travelers, adulterers and meth labs. Some travelers who cannot afford a motel opt instead to "rough it" by sleeping in a car or trailer at a highway rest stop. While this is certainly a money saver, it's not recommended, as rest stops are often frequented by transients, criminals and former members of Wham! Instead, consider these low-cost accommodation options:

- Lock self in mall restroom
- Disguise tent as art installation in modern art gallery
- Make false confession to famous unsolved crime to earn night in jail, then recant and check out

In-Room Dining

Certain kinds of American restaurants will deliver telephoned orders to your door. Chinese food restaurants cater to a clientele of depressed singles of both sexes, while pizza restaurants usually serve the prank-phone-call community. Both will be happy to deliver the wrong order of lukewarm starch to your lodging.

Luxury hotels often provide guests with a small refrigerated mini-bar stocked with alcoholic beverages and snacks. It's tempting to take something to eat or drink, especially late at night after your prostitute leaves. But it's much more economical to buy food outside the hotel and store it in your room with a small refrigerator of your own.

Emergency snack kit

Room Service

For the tired traveler who needs a hot meal or shoe shine but is too "jet lagged" or intoxicated to leave the room, most hotels offer these and other services delivered right to your door. A range of room services is available from your concierge.

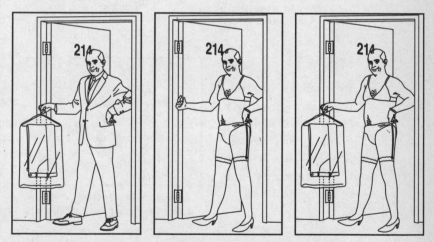

The concierge offers a wide range of services

MISCELLANEOUS INFORMATION

Cell Phones

The preferred method of communication in the United States is the cellular telephone. Americans will use their phones in situations that may seem inappropriate. Don't be concerned! Do as the locals do and use your phone whenever and wherever the spirit moves you.

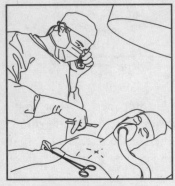

"Nothin' much, what are you doing?"

"Yeah, I'm naked too."

Mail

Be aware of the laws regulating import and export of native goods. Some things may be illegal to ship to your country, not to mention unwieldy.

Make sure to seal seams and flaps with pressure-sensitive plastic tape.

Recycling

Ecological issues have been a popular topic of discussion in America lately thanks to the activism of celebrity environmentalists like Jaguar spokesman Sting and one-time coca product fancier Don Henley. Americans show their support for these causes by purchasing as many pro-environmental products as they can afford.

Environmental activism is increasingly popular

Americans, contrary to their image as the world's most wasteful people, are dedicated to the practice of recycling. A look at the plotlines of many Hollywood blockbusters will confirm this. Recycling is also practiced in most cities, which schedule pickups of recyclable items and provide special containers for them. Be prepared to separate your recyclables by type, lest you make more work for the Sanitation Department and the roving homeless.

Green Glass

Brown Glass

Philip Glass

Specially marked bins make separating recyclables easy

Newspapers with Liberal Bias

Magazines Celebrating Soulless Materialism

Porno

Many American cities have obsolete laws on their record books that sound funny to us today. For example:

- In Flowery Beach, Georgia, it is illegal to shout "Cougar!" within city limits.

- In Baldwin Park, California, it is illegal to make a bicycle out of salami.

- In Seattle, Washington, it is illegal to maintain a monopoly in the operating system market through anticompetitive terms in your licensing and software agreements.

- In Oklahoma, doing a bad Jack Nicholson impression carries a $65 fine.

- Curiously, residents of Fedora, South Dakota, are forbidden to wear fedoras.

- Due to an early frontier border dispute, people born in West New York, New Jersey, are citizens of Finland.

- Pickup games of basketball in Fenwick, Maryland, are always shirts/skins and both teams are required to wear "old school" shorts and orthodontic headgear.

- According to a horribly outdated passage in the Constitution, nearly all Americans have a right to carry firearms.

CRIME AND SAFETY

Some visitors to the United States think America is a dangerous country filled with pistol-wielding thugs. Of course they're wrong—some Americans prefer knives, or even vials of acid. Follow these tips to avoid becoming a victim of America's mostly criminal populace or her draconian laws.

1. Narcotics are illegal in the United States, and the penalties for attempting to obtain them are steep. Be sure to bring plenty from home.

2. Do your best to look like a local. Thieves prey on tourists, and foreign visitors are easy marks with their brightly colored clothing, comically oversized backpacks, cameras strung around their necks, maps sticking out of every pocket—I mean, Jesus Christ, have you looked at yourselves?

3. Stay with your own kind. Most major American cities have a touristy area where locals never go. Whether it's San Francisco's Fisherman's Wharf, Fells Point in Baltimore or South Street Seaport in New York City, you can be sure the people milling about are tourists—just like you! Stay there and you'll have hours of safe, expensive fun in an area nothing like the city you came to visit.

FUN FACT

DID YOU KNOW...?

In America, a police officer making an arrest must inform the suspect of his Fifth Amendment rights. This law was instituted by the Supreme Court in 1966, when an accused rapist named Ernesto Miranda argued that television police dramas did not end dramatically enough.

Police

Police can be wary of foreigners—much as you would be wary of a foreigner who is not you. Here are a few simple tactics you can use to keep from being shot to death by a police officer.

1. If you are stopped for questioning by a police officer, keep your hands in plain sight. You may just be reaching for your passport, but to the sharp eye of a policeman you may appear to be grabbing a deadly bullet-shooting passport.

2. Don't startle a police officer with any unnecessary questions. A policeman is trained to make split-second decisions, and your innocent queries ("Where is the heliport?" "How much is this fine in euros?" "May I stroke your badge?") may sound like the ramblings of a crazed cop-killer reaching for a shoulder-fired rocket.

3. Don't walk too briskly away from an officer. To a police officer's super-acute perception, you could appear to be a sinister yet charismatic master criminal fleeing from the scene of a major jewel heist on your way to kidnap an heiress.

FAMILY

In order to truly experience what America has to offer, you may choose to spend part of your travels staying with a typical American family. If you do so, please notify the family in advance, so as to avoid awkward, violent situations.

Currently, there are three types of family structures in America:

❶ A single mother raising three children

❷ An abandoned child being raised by his grandmother and his step-grandfather

❸ Gay men and their adopted children

Family togetherness is obviously very important to Americans. You will often find an adult child living in his parents' spare room or basement, having moved back home in a touching illustration of filial devotion and the crash of the Internet economy. These selfless sons and daughters spend years helping their parents avoid "empty-nest syndrome" and "complete freedom and privacy." And when the child finally moves out to establish his or her own family, the parents will move in with the child when they reach retirement age and can no longer practice proper hygiene. It's apparent that American parents and children love each other so much they can't bear to be separated.

FUN FACT

DID YOU KNOW...?

If an American teenager dies, his parents will leave the room exactly the way it is? Maintaining a shrine to their beloved son or daughter seems to ease the pain of loss. If the child moves out, however, his room is turned into a den.

The Elderly

The care of the elderly has become a topic of great concern, now that scientists have discovered that most, if not all, Americans are currently growing older. The most popular way of caring for the elderly is sitting near them and listening to them rant about the Democrats.

As reported in the last census, 94% of Americans are over the age of 70. In the United States there are special homes for such people, known as "retirement communities" or "internment camps." The elderly are treated like royalty in such facilities: they are entertained, cooked for, bathed and physically and sexually abused. Family members who have relatives in nursing homes visit as much as they can, sometimes as often as once a year.

Children

Americans—specifically pop princess Whitney Houston—believe that children are the future. Unfortunately, many parents do not have enough money to support their children the way they would like. Only the wealthiest parents have the resources to send their children to exclusive boarding schools, where they will learn important skills such as squash and homosexual exploration.

Current most popular names for children in America:	Boys:	Girls:
	Trevor	Zoë
	Cody	Skylar
	Jeeves	Fiona
	Harry Potter	Radisson
	Jared	Brittany
	Jedediah	Brittney
	Ezekiel	Britney
	Deuteronomy	Brittnee
	Proverbs	B.R.T.N.Y.
	Lexus	Rachel

Pets

Pets are treated just like family members in America. You may be astonished to see pet owners giving fancy gourmet food and expensive toys to an animal that would be considered soup stock in your country, but try to understand that most Americans desire to nurture something both adorable and obedient, and their own children come up markedly short on both counts.

How to Be
a Good Guest

Be sure to show your appreciation of your host's hospitality with an appropriate gift.

No

No

Yes

FUN FACT

?

DID YOU KNOW...?
My parents wanted a girl?

When the family is fighting, often during the hours of 9am–12pm, 2pm–10pm and 3am–4am, stay quiet and do not choose sides. Also, remember to make your bed and fold all towels and linens, as your hosts would never ever do such a thing themselves.

More Guidelines

If pro-wrestling pay-per-view is shown, it is good form to chip in five bucks.

If you're invited to share a typical down-home style American meal, offer to help clean up afterward. (The styrofoam containers are usually thrown out, but ask the host what she wants to do with the extra ketchup packets.)

If the host has a teenage daughter, it is bad form to impregnate her, unless you were invited specifically for that purpose.

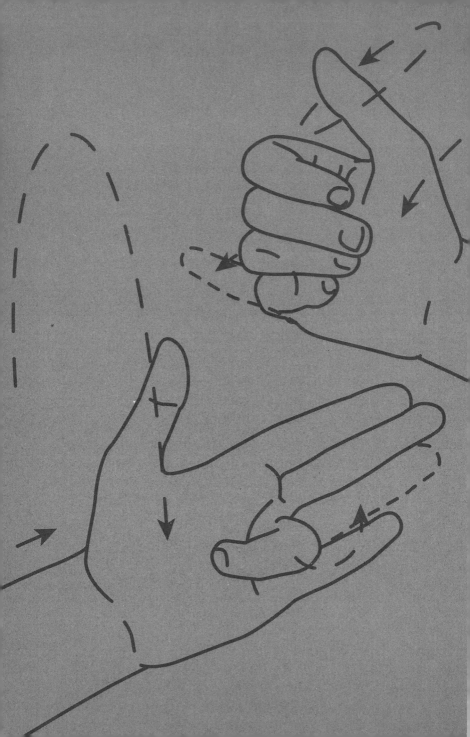

LANGUAGE AND CUSTOMS

Greetings

Americans are a friendly and gregarious people. Visitors are often surprised to find total strangers approaching them to extend greetings, such as:

- "Hey, handsome, wanna date?"
- "Have you or someone you love been injured in an accident?"
- "What you lookin' at, faggot?"

The typical greeting among Americans is the handshake, where two individuals extend and clasp right hands together, shaking them briskly up and down. Some visitors, raised on American television, attempt variations on the "soul" handshake as seen on programs such as CBS's "Good Times" and Court TV's "People v. Todd Bridges."

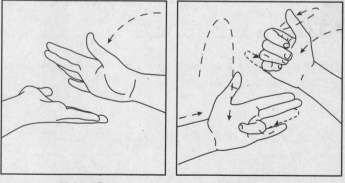

Giving "five"   The "Huggy Bear"

For popular music entertainers, the standard greeting is the "half-hug." This greeting (commonly seen on MTV), creates the appearance of closeness and affection when viewed on television, but in real life, the barest minimum of physical contact is necessary. This makes it possible for celebrities, selfish and hateful by nature, to maintain the illusion of humanity necessary to keep their fans.

Language

Many visitors who have studied the English language are surprised to find that the language spoken by Americans is less formal as well as louder and more abusive than that taught in their textbooks. In American English, the apostrophe is used liberally, usually (but not always) when a word ends in "s."

American English also makes extensive use of euphemism, profanity and slang phrases.

GLOSSARY OF COMMON ENGLISH PHRASES:

"That's fucked up!" = "That is unacceptable."

"It's the bomb!" = "It's great," or "It is a bomb."

"What's the 411?" = "What is happening on April eleventh?"

"How's it hangin'?" = "Do you find the alignment of your penis acceptable?"

"What's up with that?" or **"What's that all about?"** = "My humorous observation has no punch line."

"What the dilly, yo?" = "Pardon me, but what is the dilly?"

FUN FACT

DID YOU KNOW...?

There are over 35 million bilingual people in America, with an additional 15 million admitting to being bi-curious.

Catchphrases

Americans hate hearing vulgar language on free television, so networks replace crude swear words and offensive phrases with clever euphemisms. These expressions can be very confusing for non-natives.

CATCHPHRASE: "Sit on it!"
TRANSLATION: "Fuck you!"

CATCHPHRASE: "Up your nose with a rubber hose!"
TRANSLATION: "Fuck you sideways!"

CATCHPHRASE: "You are the weakest link. Goodbye!"
TRANSLATION: "Get the fuck out of here, you God-damn dickwad!"

CATCHPHRASE: "I did not have sexual relations with that woman."
TRANSLATION: "I received a hummer."

RELIGION

America was founded on principles of religious freedom. Also freedom from taxation, but that's another deal. Lately, many Americans are forgoing the outmoded tenets of traditional religion in favor of a belief in angels—lovable pink-cheeked cherubs with feathered wings who keep watch over those who purchase angel-related merchandise.

Judaism

Judaism remains one of America's strongest religious traditions. Its resilient culture has survived centuries of exile, widespread persecution and the tired fire-breathing act of rockin' Semite Gene Simmons.

Church of Jesus Christ of Latter Day Saints (Mormons)

Mormons are known for their clean-living lifestyles and are also notorious for the polygamy practiced by their 19th-century founders. However, Mormons would much rather be derided for their Disneyesque architecture and for the Osmonds.

Church of Scientology

Scientology is one of the few science-fiction-based religions that hasn't ended in a showy mass suicide. Yet. Some consider it a religious cult rather than a religion, but since it has a high-pressure indoctrination process and a belief system that is numbingly convoluted, it could be either. Celebrity members like John Travolta, Tom Cruise and Kirstie Alley lend credibility to the church, as everyone knows that Hollywood movie stars wouldn't get mixed up in anything flaky.

Christianity

A surprising number of Americans are practitioners of this fast-growing faith, including Oscar winner Gwyneth

Paltrow, Attorney General John Ashcroft and Gregory Hines. (Funnyman Ben Stiller is reportedly half-Christian.) Not much is known about this religion, but it seems to involve a belief in a deity named Jesus Christ and a race of corrupted elves known as Orcs.

Islam

Americans who practice Islam follow the five pillars: faith, pilgrimage, praying, fasting and explaining that they don't hate America.

Televangelism

When Americans can't come to church, church comes to them. TV preachers, or "televangelists," broadcast 24 hours a day, bringing God's message to the very sick, the very old and the very lazy. Some are faith healers and some just want to guide people into heaven, but all have an unswerving belief in helping the poor, needy and desperate spend their life savings.

HOLIDAYS

DEC. 31 / JAN. 1
New Year's Eve/
New Year's Day

American New Year's cele-brations center around Times Square in New York City, where the usual crowd of drunks, rapists and pick-pockets gather to ring in the new year the same way they have since 1904, by watch-ing the "world's oldest teenager," Dick Clark.

Dick Clark, New Year's Eve 1904

FEB. 2
Groundhog Day

American meteorological science, being somewhat less advanced than that of other nations, still forecasts weather changes by consulting small animals.

FEB. 14
Valentine's Day

On this day, lovers try to fulfill the unrealistic romantic expectations fueled by movies and television shows. Since this is impossible, the day traditionally ends in slammed doors, a cheap bouquet of flowers jammed in the garbage can and tears. Cards are also sent.

Will you be my sweet Valentine?

Please let me know ASAP, as I have some backups in mind.

I WUV OO!

Fank oo vor pudding up wiv my speesh impebiment!

To my shnuggly-wuggly eentsy-weentsy honeybaby...

I'm going to screw you so hard tonight.

A selection of popular Valentine's Day Cards

FEB. 19
Presidents' Day

The birthdays of George Washington and Abraham Lincoln have been combined into one holiday, in keeping with the American tradition of simplifying history to make it easier to remember (see sidebar on page 62).

PRESIDENTS' DAY FUN FACTS

Martin Van Buren: First president of Filipino origin

James K. Polk: Original commander of Starship Enterprise

Zachary Taylor: Invented candy ingredient known today as nougat

James Buchanan: Inspired Johnny Cash classic "Folsom Prison Blues" by shooting a man in Reno just to watch him die

Rutherford B. Hayes: Vetoed Constitutional amendment "If the van's a-rockin', don't come a-knockin'!"

Grover Cleveland: Thwarted an assassination attempt by confusing the assailant with early version of "Who's on First?" routine

William McKinley: Ended a seventy-year-long secret war with Denmark

William Howard Taft: Instituted time-honored tradition of virgin sacrifice on the White House lawn on the third Thursday of the month

Lyndon Baines Johnson: First man to hold the American presidency and the WWF Intercontinental Title simultaneously. (Though Warren Harding had both titles first, on separate occasions.)

Gerald Ford: Biological father of popular musician Morrissey

MARCH 17
St. Patrick's Day

A holiday beloved by Americans of Irish and alcoholic extraction alike. American revelers wear green clothing, drink green beer, don green plastic leprechaun hats, and get into violent, drunken green brawls, all in tribute to the man who drove the snakes out of Ireland, a callous attack on biodiversity.

MARCH / APRIL
Passover

Instead of bread, Jews eat a flat, tasteless cracker called matzoh, which they spice up with such delicacies as horseradish, gefilte fish and the slaying of the firstborn.

MAY / JUNE
Mother's Day / Father's Day

The greeting card industry created two separate days for parental appreciation. No important significance is attached to

Father's Day cards

63

the dates, or their order, except that if Mother's Day didn't come first, Father's Day would just roll over and fall asleep.

MAY
Memorial Day

Americans solemnly remember their war dead by startin' up summer with a kick-ass barbecue.

JULY 4
Independence Day

According to 76% of American college students, this holiday celebrates America's victory over Spain in the Crimean War.

SEPTEMBER
Grandparents Day

On this day (proclaimed a holiday by President Jimmy Carter in 1978), Americans pay tribute to their elderly with greeting cards, rich desserts and elaborate parties. Or, that is, they would, were they aware of the holiday's existence.

Happy Grandparents Day, Granddad!

Here's to four or five more!

OCT. 31
Halloween

On this day American children follow up the phrase "Trick or Treat" with a variety of rhymes: "Smell my feet," "Give me something good to eat," "I'm a vegan; please no meat," "Preferably some untilled wheat."

NOV. 11
Veterans Day

This day honors those who fought in America's wars. It differs from Memorial Day in that the honorees are still alive and able to realize that people are ignoring them the rest of the year.

NOVEMBER
Thanksgiving Day

Americans observe this harvest festival by eating an obscene amount of food, so it may be hard to tell it from a regular day. Look for the hand-outline turkey pictures on the fridge.

NOVEMBER
Election Day

Around this time of year, America's largest political parties distribute aggressive propaganda throughout the country. Some samples from a recent election:

DEC. 25
Christmas

Christmas celebrates the birth of Jesus Christ. Some traditionalists bemoan the glitzy commercialism of the

modern American Christmas and wish they could bring the holiday back to its roots, when the Grinch was still just an animated character and Santa Claus drank Coke from a bottle instead of a can.

Christmas cards

WORK

Many foreigners who use their government-mandated six weeks of paid vacation time to visit America are surprised at how hard Americans work. This willingness to put in long hours at the office is both a legacy of the Puritan colonists' Protestant work ethic and an antidote to unpleasant domestic situations.

The sixteen-hour workday may be an American tradition dating back to, well, before labor unions, but the concept of "multi-tasking" is new. Technology has made it possible for an employee to do two or three jobs at the same time while only being paid for one. This saves the employer money, and the savings are reinvested in the economy in the form of extra-large tips for the employer's maid, personal trainer and yacht captain.

American employers are proud of their motivational skills. Some reward workers with snacks or even coffee sold at a very reasonable price. Others post an "Employee of the Month" plaque in a prominent spot so that customers can recognize and pay tribute to the honored worker during the eleven seconds their fast-food transaction will last. Many employers encourage good-natured competition among their workers, in which the best performers are rewarded with continued employment.

In some workplaces, the work environment is made more attractive with on-site facilities like cafeterias, daycare centers and showers to eliminate the profit loss that occurs when workers leave the area to eat, raise their children or clean themselves.

FUN FACT

DID YOU KNOW...?

Most American children say they want to be a fireman, a ballerina or an astronaut when they grow up. But then they grow up and they're all, like, "I'm gonna be Senior Project Manager, Midwest Division."

Many American employers designate the last day of the week as "Casual Friday." This is a morale-building exercise where employees are encouraged to "let their hair down" by wearing khakis instead of a business suit.

Even on Casual Friday, clients will expect businesslike attire

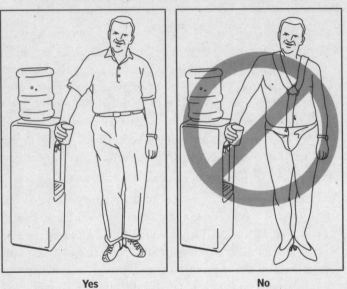

Yes   No

American attitudes toward work are reflected in this popular newspaper strip that can be found tacked onto cubicle walls all over the country.

GILBERT   **by Adam Scott**

GILBERT, TODAY I'M GOING TO WORK YOU TOO HARD AND HOLD A BORING, POINTLESS MEETING TO INSPIRE YOUR WRY OBSERVATIONS!

LOOKS LIKE SOMEONE JUST HIRED A CONSULTANT.

I AM A FOOL! ALL BOSSES ARE! I LOOK GOOD ON A MUG OR CALENDAR!

Americans love to read books, as long as the books promise
to teach them how to make money. This rules out *Ethan
Frome*, but explains the thousands of business books
published every year. Here are some bestsellers:

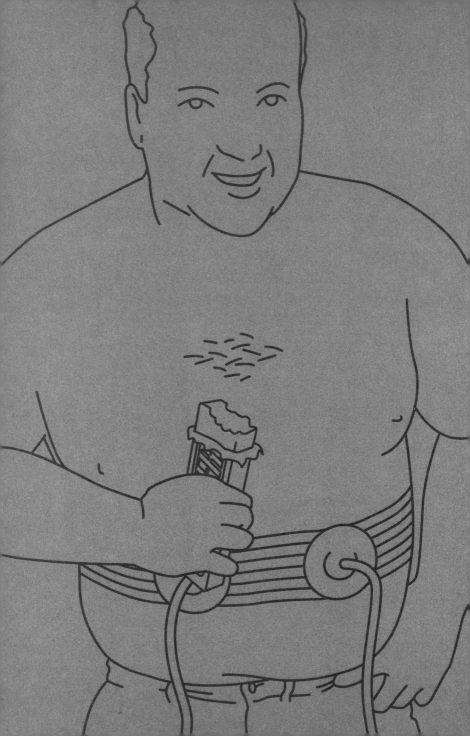

HEALTH

Unlike many other countries, America has no national health care system. When Americans become sick or injured, they don't wait in a long line to see a doctor. Instead, they use good old American know-how to treat themselves. A simple trip to the corner store will provide all the first-aid supplies you might need:

HEADACHE: aspirin, ibuprofen
BODY/MUSCLE ACHE: Scotch, highballs
HEARTACHE: "The Songs of Leonard Cohen" CD

WEIGHT LOSS

The typical American is always looking for ways to stay slim without having to participate in the unpleasant sweaty activity usually associated with losing weight.

Electrotherapy

Americans have figured out how to exercise in their sleep! Electrotherapy devices tone muscles by jolting them with short, sharp bolts of electricity. Unlike traditional exercise, this regimen of painful muscle spasms can be done while enjoying a tasty snack.

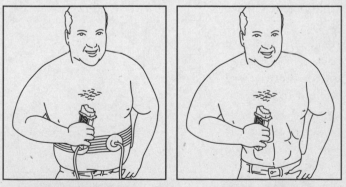

Before electrotherapy   After electrotherapy

Fat Blockers

Many American mail-order companies sell revolutionary medicines called "fat blockers." These tablets purport to allow the taker to eat as much food as she desires without having to worry about weight gain. However, the molten "blocked" fat is forcibly and uncontrollably expelled from the body through the anus. No one said weight loss would be pretty!

FUN FACT

DID YOU KNOW...?

There were 5.7 million elective cosmetic surgery procedures done in America this year, only half of which were performed on actor Mickey Rourke.

SPECIALIZED MEDICINE

Chiropractors

Many Americans regularly visit a type of health practitioner called a chiropractor. Chiropractic science is easy to understand. If you have back or neck pain, a chiropractor will attempt to relieve it through a rigorous back massage. If you have migraine headaches, the chiropractor will fix that with a back massage.

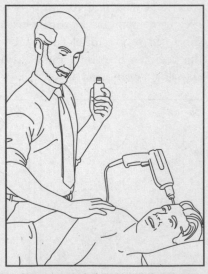

Chiropractor helping injured patient

Concussion? Gunshot wound? Back massage.

DISTINGUISHING THE CHIROPRACTOR FROM THE EROTIC MASSEUSE

LOCATION
CHIROPRACTOR: Office building in business area of town
EROTIC MASSEUSE: Platinum Fantasy Spa and Private Club, near the airport

NAME
CHIROPRACTOR: "Dr. Stephen Jones"
EROTIC MASSEUSE: "Monique"

IN WAITING ROOM
CHIROPRACTOR: pamphlets ("Subluxation and You"); outdated health, travel, and fashion magazines; other clients who avoid eye contact
EROTIC MASSEUSE: other clients who avoid eye contact

APPAREL
CHIROPRACTOR: white lab coat over business suit
EROTIC MASSEUSE: thong

SERVICES OFFERED
CHIROPRACTOR: "Correction of vertebral misalignment"
EROTIC MASSEUSE: "Nude reverse," "Body slide," "Shower reverse deluxe massage and show," "Royal VIP combo," "Deluxe reverse with two ladies"

ATTEMPTS TO FIND OUT IF YOU'RE A COP?
CHIROPRACTOR: no
EROTIC MASSEUSE: yes

ATTEMPTS TO FIND OUT IF YOUR INSURANCE PROVIDER COVERS THIS TREATMENT?
CHIROPRACTOR: yes
EROTIC MASSEUSE: no

DISPASSIONATE, CLINICAL ATTITUDE WHILE MANIPULATING YOUR BODY PARTS?
CHIROPRACTOR: yes
EROTIC MASSEUSE: yes

heroin aficionado

MARCH 2002 ▪ $6.95

FOR THE JUNKIE WHO APPRECIATES THE FINER THINGS

Mainlining vs. Skin-Popping
The Aficionado Poll

Does Junk Age You Prematurely?
Supermodel Sabrina Caravella Debunks the Rumors

NEWS MEDIA

Newspapers

In America, newspapers are found in every town, from the metropolis (Los Angeles, CA) to the small village (Fancy Gap, VA) to the imaginary forest (Elvenhalls of Mirkwood, northern Middle-Earth). Local newspapers provide in-depth coverage of regional events as well as opinionated commentaries by arrogant, uninformed school board members. America's national newspaper, *USA Today*, is a full-color periodical featuring short articles and explanatory graphs that cater to Americans' tiny attention spans and predisposition toward shiny things.

TABLOIDS: Tabloids are newspapers that focus on stories too racy, too sensational and too untrue for the traditional news media. They are unmatched in their coverage of fantastic events involving spacemen, Sasquatch and celebrity "shockers," "blow-ups" and "abortions."

Typically sensational tabloid headlines

FUN FACT

DID YOU KNOW...?

Powerful newspaper titan William Randolph Hearst invented the sensationalist techniques that came to be called "yellow journalism." He is said to have once wired a correspondent, "You furnish the pictures and I'll furnish the war." Yet all he really wanted was the wooden sled he loved as a child.

Magazines

Americans are the world's biggest magazine consumers. A visit to a typical American newsstand will reveal hundreds of niche titles catering to every possible hobby on a staggering array of paper stocks.

If you plan to pick up more than a couple of magazines while in America, be prepared to do some heavy lifting! Many American magazines are surprisingly hefty in size, just like the people who make them.

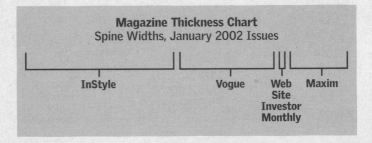

TV News

Most Americans get their news through television because it offers the same excitement as a major motion picture, complete with bombastic John Williams theme music. Although TV news bureaus are widely criticized for reporting only the most shocking events, many balance their coverage with advertisements for life insurance, burglar alarms and sleeping pills. Americans have also pioneered the concept of "good news"—news programs that avoid dwelling on gloomy foreign conflicts and baffling financial minutiae in favor of uplifting stories about the lives of popular entertainers, cooking demonstrations and clips of cute puppies helping out at soup kitchens.

FUN FACT

?

DID YOU KNOW...?

Some American television personalities publish magazines based on their personas and aimed at their audience. For example, "O" is put out by Oprah Winfrey, "Rosie" is helmed by Rosie O'Donnell, "Macworld" celebrates tennis great John McEnroe's lifestyle and philosophy, and "Vanity Fair" is published by Prince protege and nasty girl Vanity.

TRANSPORTATION

Driving

Americans love to drive. Given a choice between a healthful four-minute walk to the corner grocery store or getting in the car, cranking up the stereo and speeding to an identical store four states away, an American will drive every time.

The most popular American automobile is the Sport Utility Vehicle. You may be more familiar with them as "tanks" or "anti-personnel vehicles." Besides allowing motorists to sublimate their fears of

Sport Utility Vehicle

penile inadequacy, SUVs are great for "off-roading"—that is, when their narrow wheelbase and high center of gravity tip them off the road and over an embankment, they can roll and roll with minimal damage to the vehicle's resale value.

Another popular American transport is the motorcycle. American-made "hogs" like the Harley-Davidson were once associated almost exclusively with leather-jacketed outlaw motorcycle gangs. Today they have been co-opted by leather-jacketed Hollywood actors who can afford to pay for custom parts as well as for the pricey head injuries and crushed pelvises.

As a visitor, your vehicle choice is limited to what an agency has available for rental. Still, you're sure to find a car you like, whether you're interested in a red Geo Metro, a white Geo Metro or a purple metal-flake Geo Metro.

Driving Defensively

American drivers have turned driving from a mundane means of getting from point A to point B into an exhilarating adventure by eliminating the "buzzkill" that is personal responsibility.

American citizens are eligible for a driver's license at age 16, and can keep that license well into old age, provided they are alive and no more than 80% blind. Because of their charmingly happy-go-lucky approach to motor vehicle operation, Americans frequently find themselves involved in collisions. If you pass an accident on the road, it is customary to show respect for the injured victims by slowing to a crawl and staring at the carnage with avid curiosity on your face. Your reduction in speed will help drivers behind you get a good look as well. Be sure to ask the police and rescue workers questions like "Any trouble, officer?" and "Hey, anyone get decapitated?" They appreciate a chance to chat while on duty.

Speed Limits

American highways are marked with "Speed Limit" signs that suggest a maximum safe driving speed. However, the posted speed limit is far below the actual (secret) speed limit. Always add 20 to 30 miles per hour to the posted speed limit in order to keep up with the flow of traffic and reinforce your "outlaw" status.

FUN FACT

Americans love to make their feelings known with a variety of stickers on their car bumpers.

"I don't drink and drive—except when I do!"

"My honor student had sex with your honor student"

"I brake when I come to a red light"

"Proud parent of a child"

"Don't blame me—I don't vote or get involved in politics in any way"

"Keep your laws off my heroin supply"

Traffic Signs

American traffic signs can sometimes be difficult to fathom. Common signs like "Stop" or "One Way" are fairly self-explanatory, but others may require translation:

 The figures holding square black bags indicate that the driver should slow down, as there is a Kate Spade sale occurring nearby.

 "R x R" means "rest and relaxation." At areas where this sign is posted, you may park your car for a relaxing nap.

 The image of a car followed by wavy black lines marks an area where the road has been certified conducive for swerving and braking suddenly, leaving cool skid marks.

 This protest sign can be found just beyond many street and highway improvement sites. If you see it, honk your horn in support of the anti–road work movement.

 This, of course, is a sign informing you of the speed limit on the interstate. Don't forget, that's 95 miles, not kilometers, per hour!

 This sign uses an alternate spelling of "car" to remind you to use your car while passing other vehicles. Like many American warning signs and labels, it may seem unnecessary, but it protects the Federal Highway Administration from lawsuits brought by daredevils on foot or horseback.

This sign prohibits all wordless gestures of encouragement and approval, which can be distracting for drivers.

 This sign warns you to be alert, as learning-disabled children are afoot.

Driving under the influence of alcohol is illegal in America. Americans looking to cause car accidents instead use their cell phones and change CDs in the player while driving.

No   Yes

Being Pulled Over

If you see flashing red lights in your rear-view mirror and hear a repetitive high-pitched whine, you have either driven into a Chuck E. Cheese restaurant or are being signaled to pull over by the police. Police detainment can occur for any number of reasons. Perhaps your vehicle just has a burned-out tail light or an expired registration sticker. Or maybe the officer has not made his monthly arrest quota and is going to frame you for a crime you did not commit.

One problem that Americans are experiencing more frequently in recent years is that of "racial profiling." The problem is often referred to as "DWB—Driving While Black" or "DWODB—Driving While Ol' Dirty Bastard."

Public Transit

In the last few decades, the rising cost of gasoline and a growing environmental awareness have resulted in an increased interest in public transportation. Interest, that is, not ridership. Most Americans would still rather drive than get on a crowded, smelly subway or a rickety city bus, but they think it's a very good idea for other people to use public transportation. Every day, from the comfortable back seats of their chauffeur-driven limousines, American public officials sign legislation mandating tens of dollars to the improvement of public transit.

Subway

Most major American cities are linked by underground railroads called "subways." While documentary films like "Death Wish" may make you hesitant to ride a city subway, the truth is that the systems are mostly safe. The muggers and rapists who terrorized subway riders in the '70s have been replaced by friendly (if leprotic) beggars, high-decibel religious zealots and street performers. These days, the glancing blow you feel to the side of your head is less likely to be from the truncheon of a pickpocket than from the sneaker of a breakdancing teen.

During busy commute hours, subways can become crowded, and male riders customarily relinquish seats for the infirm, the elderly and the beautiful. If a subway car's doors begin to close before you can get into the car, do not hold or pry open the doors. Most system delays are caused by individuals trying to hold the trains to a personal timetable. If you find yourself stuck between the doors, be calm. The doors will open up eventually.

Be patient

Because maintaining customer restrooms would be far too costly, the walls, benches and stairwells inside all subway stations have been designated as public urinals. Urinating from the platform, however, is inadvisable, due to the possibility of electrocution by contact with the third rail. And as much as you may like the subway system, you really don't want to wind up as a "conductor"! (Conductors and other transit employees earn low wages.)

FUN FACT

DID YOU KNOW...?

Many people think that Henry Ford invented the automobile, but that's not quite accurate. What he really invented was a time machine that allowed him to steal the idea for automobiles from the future.

Buses

Buses are both inexpensive and inefficient—key attractions to the poor, the very young and the elderly, none of whom need to worry about the concept of being "on time."

Almost all American towns are served by city bus lines. For a nominal charge, these buses will pick you up from a spot a great distance from where you are, and whisk you miles away to a spot that's not really very close to where you want to be. Some lines even offer free bus travel—"free" buses are notable for their bright yellow color and ridership of small children. Hop on board! Though the seats are small, the price can't be beat.

Trains

Visitors from overseas who are used to efficient, speedy national train service will feel right at home in America as long as they never go near a train.

Bicycling

Bicycling in the big city is a quick, efficient way to get to any number of places, including the park and the emergency room. You will find that American drivers are very courteous to bikers and will often drive slowly alongside you as you pedal, blaring their horns in a friendly manner and jokingly threatening to run you off the road.

Statistically, bicycling in an American city is even safer than taking a bath in your own home while operating an electric belt sander. But to be absolutely safe, it's best to keep these rules in mind:

Be sure to wear a helmet. In most states it is required by law, and it affords your head protection in even the most grisly accidents.

Adequate protection

Recent studies have shown that bike riding can cause impotency. Make sure to procreate before purchasing or approaching a bicycle.

Make sure you can be seen in low or dim light. Drivers who are intoxicated or asleep have difficulty seeing bicyclists. Wear clothing that guarantees you will be noticed.

Proper cycling attire: Make sure you can be seen

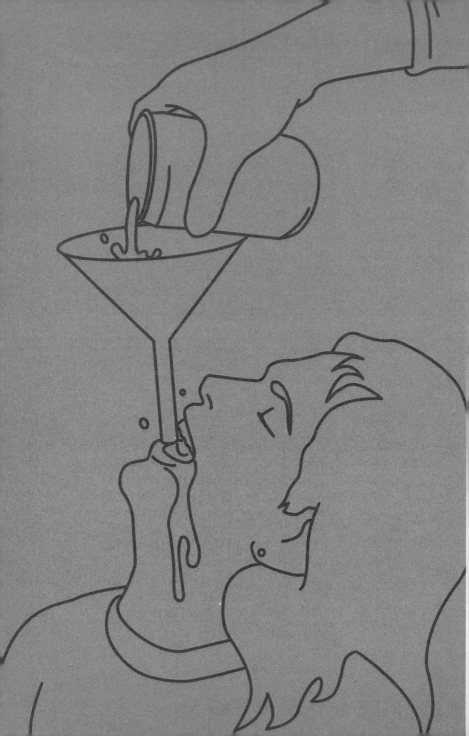

DRUGS AND ALCOHOL

America is known worldwide for its stiff anti-drug laws. It's best to remember this before trying to obtain any contraband substance. Is a marijuana cigarette worth a two-month stretch in prison? No, but a half-pound brick of hash or a kilo of uncut cocaine might be. Use your judgment.

In major metropolitan areas, illegal drugs are often openly sold in public parks and "slum" areas. Walking through such an area, you may hear individuals surreptitiously offer you drugs by whispering their slang names of "bud," "smoke," "crack," "smack" or "blow." Marijuana is known variously as "weed," "bud," "grass," "dope," "fisherman's blues," "Wilford Brimley's Special Oatmeal," "Morris Day and the Time," "Purina hippie chow," "the fifth Beatle," "the way to San Jose" and "Los Angeles Laker Kobe Bryant." Listen carefully, for not all slang terms refer to hard drugs.

"Time?"

Not offering drugs

"Agua fresca?"

May be offering drugs

"Wanna buy some drugs?"

May be offering drugs

Many Americans avoid the illegality of street drugs by having their narcotics prescribed by a physician. If you crave the euphoria only a handful of codeine pills can provide, you might want to try breaking a leg or hip bone. Your physician will be only too happy to prescribe you some of those precious snow-white tablets of joy.

The most controversial American prescription drug today is Viagra. Popular with elderly men, these sky-blue pills give the patient the steely erection of a nineteen-year-old boy. Unfortunately, it is still attached to the user's wrinkly, withered seventy-something body.

Another common prescription medicine is the anti-depressant. These pills are prescribed not only for crippling depression but for a wide range of recently discovered illnesses such as Social Anxiety Disorder, Reality Discontent Syndrome and Unavoidable Slight Disappointment Disease.

Alcohol

While they may look down upon illegal drug users, Americans love a drunk. The humorous alcoholic is a popular archetype in American entertainment both on and off the screen.

America's love affair with the lovable/hot drunk.

American beer is different from its foreign counterpart. Unlike the crisp, golden lagers and rich, dark stouts you may be familiar with, American beer is known less for its flavor than for its appallingly sexist advertising and affordability in large quantities.

When identifying American beers, it is helpful to learn the nicknames by which these popular brands are known. Budweiser, for example, is generally referred to by the diminutive "Bud." Pabst Blue Ribbon is best known by its acronym "PBR," while beers such as Coors Light, Schaefer, Schlitz, Lucky Lager, Falstaff, Michelob, Milwaukee's Best, Schmidt's, Miller Light, Miller High Life and Miller Genuine Draft are referred to collectively as "swill," "ass-beer," or "piss." Unlike the urine it resembles, however, American beer is almost always served ice-cold.

In bars, you may hear people ask for drinks with wittily risqué names like "Fuzzy Navel," "Sex on the Beach" and "Zima." These delicious cocktails are very popular with the younger crowd, as consuming them makes one both drunk and effeminate.

College

Drinking is very popular among college students, as evidenced by the T-shirts seen on American campuses.

The most popular alcohol at American universities is beer, often served out of metallic barrels known as kegs. Students are always finding new, creative ways to ingest beer.

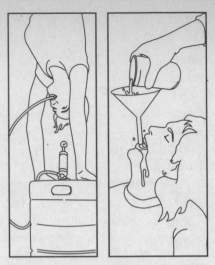

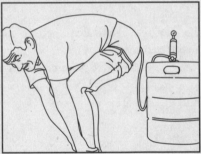

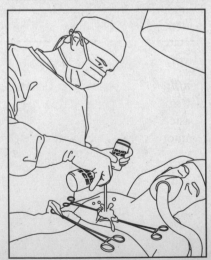

Rehabilitation

If you feel that you've inadvertently acquired a "habit" and can't stop abusing alcohol or narcotics, don't worry! America is the world capital of support groups and twelve-step programs. There are groups in America to help with just about every problem you can think of and some you might not imagine, including Overeaters Anonymous, Sex Addicts Anonymous, Adult Children of Eddie Fisher and Parents and Friends of Crack Whores.

ALTERNATIVES

People looking to achieve the euphoria, blackened teeth and foul breath of a hardened drug addict without risking incarceration turn to these safe alternatives to illegal narcotics.

Tobacco

CIGARETTE SMOKING is a habit enjoyed by many Americans, as it is relaxing and looks "cool." Most smokers are persuaded to start by macho advertising images of rugged sportsmen, mustachioed cowboys and dick-faced cartoon camels.

There are a few cigarette varieties available in America:

Filtered cigarettes are tipped with a cylinder of cellulose or acetate fibers that filters out most of the cigarette's tobacco flavor, replacing it with hot acetate fumes.

Unfiltered cigarettes don't have a filter, and are preferred by smokers who don't want the rich natural flavor of toasted tobacco adulterated with anything but nicotine, ammonia, chemical glues and binders.

Menthol cigarettes are suffused with the same peppermint-based substance used in popular cough drops, perfect for anyone seeking a cigarette to soothe the very afflictions it causes.

In California, smoking is prohibited in bars and nightclubs, as California's drinkers and Ecstasy users are extremely health-conscious.

CIGARS have enjoyed a brief resurgence in popularity among celebrities, as the abhorrent stench repels all but the most sycophantic admirers. In America, enthusiasts of cigar smoking are known as "aficionados" or "assholes."

FUN FACT

?

DID YOU KNOW...?

43% of Americans live solely on the income from tobacco lawsuits.

Coffee

Americans drink coffee as a morning "pick-me-up"— the caffeine in coffee is a stimulant, obviating the old-fashioned ritual of eight hours of sleep per night. Many workplaces offer free coffee in lieu of "breaks" or vacation time. A number of coffee franchises have popped up all over America, supplanting the "corner dealer" of old.

ABOVE: Yesterday
BELOW: Today

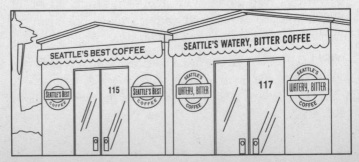

CUISINE

Italy has pasta and Mexico the enchirito, but don't count America out! American ingenuity has provided the world with many unique foodstuffs:

Common American Foods

❶ Oreo cookie cereal   ❹ Breakfast-stuffed "Crescent Roll™"
❷ Pudding in a can   ❺ Fruit-colored corn syrup patties
❸ Spiced meat wands   ❻ Pizza-infused fried dough

Americans buy their food in giant warehouses called "supermarkets." Foodstuffs are packed onto metal shelves arranged in long aisles, just narrow enough for 1.5 carts to fit through. The resulting "traffic jams" give people time to browse and notice items they may not otherwise have seen.

U.S.-Only Foods

Visitors may be perplexed by the strange packages and unfamiliar brand names staring back at them from American grocery store shelves. The contents of some packages are not immediately discernable from their names.

RANCH DRESSING: A misnomer, as it has nothing to do with ranches. It is instead a viscous white substance that, while dairy-based, is neither milk nor cheese. It is usually poured on salads to help negate their nutritional value.

BUFFALO WINGS: Not made from buffalo at all, but rather small chicken wings deep-fried in a spicy red batter, usually available warm from the supermarket's "deli" section, a favorite of sports fans, bachelors and alcoholics.

BUTTER BUDS: Freeze-dried butter-flavored granules, which when added to food gives it the flavor of Butter Buds.

RESTAURANTS

You can tell America has a rich and diverse cuisine by observing Americans' enormous girth. Though many Americans occasionally enjoy the exotic foreign delights that can be obtained at restaurants like the Olive Garden, most subsist on delicious native food. You can sample American cuisine inexpensively from innumerable nationwide chains, sometimes served in a traditional colorful box with toy.

Destination Restaurants

Restaurants that combine food and entertainment are an American specialty. You've probably heard of such famous American establishments as Planet Hollywood and the Hard Rock Café, where you can enjoy a variety of mediocre foods underneath Jean-Claude Van Damme's underpants or Neal Schon's guitar. Many large cities have "fifties"-themed diners, where you can be transported back in time to a more innocent era where girls in poodle skirts "went steady" with boys suspected of communist sympathies and hamburgers cost nine dollars.

"Theme" restaurants cater to the fantasy that one might run into a real, live celebrity when visiting. Of course, the closest an actual celebrity gets to a theme restaurant is an investor meeting. Still, these establishments provide an opportunity for the average person to experience celebrity-caliber dining. At the many sports-themed restaurants (like ESPNZone) you can dine on bacon cheeseburgers, mozzarella sticks and mimosas just like a real American sports star in training.

Fast Food

Fast food has become synonymous with American cuisine. A typical fast food establishment, as the name suggests, is geared toward speed. To that end, most have only a few items on the menu, all of which can be prepared quickly and easily, or changed into new items with the addition of bacon or American cheese.

For a nominal fee, most fast food meals can be "supersized." When you request a "super-sized" order, the standard size beverage and side dish is replaced with a much larger portion. This is a good option for the budget-minded person or the suicidal diabetic.

ABOVE:
Standard
portion
RIGHT:
Supersized
portion

P.J. Mc O'MULLICUDDY'S

Saloon, Tavern, Beer Hall, Pub & Olde-Tyme Deep Fryery

APPETIZERS

Batter Bonanza

Deep-Fried Cracklin' Nuggets
Spicy Fried Batter Fingers
Krispy-Dipt™ Flav-R-Strips
With our Olde-Tyme
Ranch-Style Dippin' Sauce
$6.75

FOR THE KIDS

P.J.'s Happy Lunch

Hot Dog
Bag of Chips
Lite Beer
Toy Prize
$4.50

DESSERTS

Sweet-E-Pie

Crushed off-brand chocolate
creme-filled sandwich cookies
smothered in rich maple syrup
and sprinkled with coconut
$6.75

Creme Filling
$1.25

P.J.'S LUNCH FAVORITES

Bacon Grande $5.75
One pound of the very freshest American bacon, sliced thick,
dripping with Ranch dressing and topped with melted
Cheddar, served on buttered white bread.

Halfa Heifer $52.99
One half of a juicy Hereford cow, served hot and steamy on a
garlic sesame bun. With home fries, add .75.

Businessman's Quickie $8.50
Ice-cold Thermos™ filled with P.J.'s extra-dry Martini mix,
served with roll of breath mints. You keep the Thermos™!

Dieter's De-Lite $3.99
A crisp, cool leaf of your favorite lettuce (choice of Romaine,
Iceberg or Butter) and a cup of our tangy lite mayonnaise.

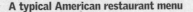

FEELING LOW?
Not for long! What you need is one of
P.J.'s patented pick-me-ups – now
guaranteed not to cause blindness!

Chocolate Margarita $3.99
Gin 'n' Jell-O $1.89
Banana & Beer Cooler $3.99

A typical American restaurant menu

McDonald's

The largest American fast food chain is McDonald's.
McDonald's is an especially popular restaurant with
children, who are drawn to the restaurant's cartoon
mascots—a bubble-coiffed clown, a fuzzy purple blob and
an escaped felon. Children also enjoy the "Happy Meal," so
named because the mini hamburger, small french fry
serving and plastic toy cost a tiny fraction of the price of the
meal, and that makes stockholders very happy indeed.

McDonald's cashiers are aided by state-of-the-art cash registers to help increase efficiency and reduce the need for costly skilled labor. These registers don't have a numerical keypad, but a special keypad with pictographic symbols representing each available menu item. When you order a "Big Mac," the cashier presses the "Big Mac" button. If you order a chocolate milkshake, the clerk presses the "chocolate shake" button. If you ask for the restroom key, the clerk presses his hands against his temples in frustration.

Because of their fanatical concern for customer safety, McDonald's food packaging has been amended to notify customers that McDonald's food is not only fun, it's also dangerous:

WARNING: THE CONTENTS OF THIS CUP MAY SCALD YOUR GENITALS.

DO NOT REACH INTO THE OIL FOR YOUR FRIES. LET US PACKAGE THEM FOR YOU.

McDonaldland Cookies

Enriched wheat flour (niacin, reduced iron, thiamine mononitrate (vitamin B1), riboflavin (vitamin B2), folic acid), sugar, vegetable shortening (partially hydrogenated soybean and/or cottonseed oil), high fructose corn syrup. Contains 2% or less of salt, baking powder (sodium acid pyrophosphate, sodium bicarbonate, monocalcium phosphate), soybean lecithin, natural flavor (vegetable source). (may contain traces of peanuts).

WARNING: FOR EXTERNAL USE ONLY.

RIGHT: McDonald's packaging warns the unsuspecting consumer of hidden dangers

KFC

Until recently, this fast food chain was known as "Kentucky Fried Chicken." Because of modern customers' negative associations with deep frying and Kentucky, the chain decided to shorten its name to an association-free three-letter acronym. Unlike most chains, which are represented by fictional mascots, KFC's mascot is the very real Colonel Harlan Sanders, a flamboyantly goateed Southerner who since 1980 has represented KFC from the grave.

Taco Bell

The Taco Bell chain specializes in foods made from different combinations of lettuce, grated cheese, re-hydrated refried beans and ground beef, to which it assigns made-up Spanish names.

TOP LEFT: The Chalupa
TOP RIGHT: The Enchirito
BOTTOM LEFT: La Catastrofe Grande

Street Vendors

Busy Americans love to dine alfresco on cuisine prepared by chefs who have nowhere to wash their hands in a facility unprotected from car exhaust, flying insects and pigeon droppings.

In the mornings these carts offer coffee, muffins, and bagels, and in the afternoons they adjust their offerings to hot dogs, sausages,

ICE COLD
Clam Goulash

THE PRIDE OF ST. LOUIS
Clam Goulash

St. Louis regional foodstuffs

E.coli and hepatitis-C. Sometimes these carts also feature popular regional foodstuffs like Boston Baked Pie and Georgia's "Peanut Buster Parfait."

Less-Fast Food

Sometimes called "sit down" restaurants, these establishments combine the rudimentary cuisine and minimal atmosphere of the fast food restaurant with the comfortable chairs and dim lighting of more costly eateries. Many sit down restaurants are open around the clock. This makes them a popular haunt of marijuana-addled teens, who often congregate at such establishments after getting "wasted." These giggling, red-eyed youths can often be seen between 12 and 3am, huddled over a shared plate of french fries, nachos or french-fried nachos, or managing the restaurant.

When entering a sit down establishment you should be mindful of visual cues that will tell you the level of dignity you can expect during your meal.

**No Shirt
No Shoes
NO SERVICE!**

A holdover from the "hippie" days of the 1970s, this sign indicates that patrons not wearing a shirt or appropriate footwear will be refused service at this establishment. These rules still apply.

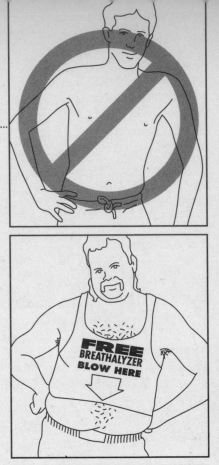

TOP: Improper attire
CENTER: Proper attire
BOTTOM: Also acceptable

IN GOD WE TRUST
ALL OTHERS PAY CASH!

This sign indicates that credit cards and checks are not acceptable forms of payment, unless you have suitable identification proving you are God, in which case a personal check is probably fine.

Where you see this sign posted, cigarette smoking may be enjoyed before or after your meal in the parking lot outside.

No   Yes

Though there are literally hundreds of regional variations, some of the more popular American "sit down" restaurants are:

Denny's

Denny's restaurants are best known for their breakfast menu, featuring the "Original Grand Slam," "Moons Over My Hammy" and other things you may be embarrassed to utter. Regardless of which "slam" you choose, your meal will consist of an obscenely large mound of cured, fried meats, fried potatoes and fried or scrambled eggs. Diet-conscious diners may enjoy a simple cup of coffee and a cigarette with employees in the parking lot.

T.G.I. Friday's

T.G.I. Friday's derives its name from the acronym TGIF, which stands for "Thank Goodness It's Friday" or for those working in the kitchen, "The Grill Is Filthy." (The chain's original acronym, G.D.I.O.T. stood for "God Damn, It's Only Tuesday!") T.G.I. Friday's is known for its "crazy" décor; its walls are covered with old license plates, metal signs, antiquated sporting equipment and other novelty items, providing the mouth-watering atmosphere of a junk shop or musty basement.

The extroverted behavior of Friday's wait staff can seem inappropriately forward to someone from a more reserved culture.

Hooters

Hooters, named for its distinctive owl mascot, is one of the most rapidly growing restaurant chains in America.

The buxom waitstaff at Hooters wear tight-fitting bosom-enhancing uniforms specially designed to cloud the minds of male patrons, leading them to unwittingly order expensive appetizers and numerous alcoholic beverages.

Standard Restaurant	**Hooters Restaurant**

"No thank you, I'm not interested in any potato skins this evening."	"Why, I'd love another banana daiquiri!"

If for some reason you should be assigned a waitress with small breasts, feel free to let that be reflected in your tip.

20% tip	**8% tip**	**Call security**

ADDITIONAL POINTERS

Bread and Water

At most American restaurants, ice water and a plate of bread are offered free of charge to diners upon being seated. Don't fill up! You'll feel pretty silly walking out without paying.

"How Is Everything?"

It is an American custom for your waitperson to come to your table at various points through the meal and ask "How is everything?" Like the American greeting "How are you?" it is not to be taken literally. While they are required to ask, your server really does not care to hear your opinion, and will try to time his/her visit to coincide with your mouth being full of food. A simple nod or "thumbs up" sign will make them go away.

Dessert

After the remnants of your meal are taken away, you will be offered a dessert menu. Most American desserts are cakes made with some combination of chocolate, candy bars and adjectives. Two examples are the Chocoholic Oh Henry Meringue Mud Pie  and the Sinfully Cocoa Caramel Fudge Almond Roca Turtle Truffle Cake. Most of these desserts can be enjoyed with whipped "crème" (French for "non-dairy dessert topping") or "à la mode" (French for "add a dollar").

Paying and Gratuities

After dessert you will be presented with a small leatherette portfolio. This is not a gift, but rather a protective folder that contains your bill. If you are dining with a large group, you should argue over who owes how much, and then leave an unsorted pile of bills and coins on the table as you leave.

As paying a living wage to the waitstaff is optional in America, it has become customary for sympathetic customers to leave behind a healthy gratuity and a pleasant smile. Using the below chart, calculating the proper tip amount is simple:

A. BASE RATE: 15%	B. WAITER ATTITUDE SURLY -4 FRIENDLY +2 DRUNK -2	C. WAITER APPEARANCE HOT +3 SLOPPY -1 DAMP -3	D. FOOD ORDERED APPETIZER +1 ENTRÉE +2 DESSERT +1	E. DEGREE OF DIFFICULTY Rate from 0.0 to 10.0, divide by 10 and add to total	F. SUBTOTAL Total boxes A-E

		Multiply or divide total from box F with all that apply below:	
1.	Waitperson refills your cup with coffee	x 1.675	
2.	Problem is, your cup was filled with orange juice	÷ 2.5	
3.	Waitperson calls you "hon"	x 1.224	
4.	Waitperson calls you "cheap-ass"	÷ 4.357	
5.	Waitperson calls you at home	call police	
6.	Are you at Denny's?	÷ 1.397	
7.	Mints left with check	x 1.445	
8.	Waitperson left with your credit card	call police	
	Subtotal from boxes 1–8:		
	Multiply by local sales tax, divide subsequent figure by 6:		
	YOUR TIP:		

Although it may be common practice in some countries, in America you should refrain from setting out a plate of money at the beginning of the meal with a cardboard sign reading "Your tip," and then gradually removing money from that plate as problems arise.

ENTERTAINMENT

Music

American popular music can be heard booming from trendy clothing boutiques, inside sport utility vehicles, and through the paper-thin walls of your hotel room. A Discman or MP3 player is a wise investment, as it allows you to listen only to your choice of music, and drowns out disagreeable loud noises common in American cities (honking car horns, screams for help, the Dave Matthews Band).

Movies

The moviegoing experience is quite different here than in your country. Americans like their movies LOUD. In fact, in most multiplexes, it's possible to hear the noisier parts of the movie being shown in the adjacent theatre. Don't worry, though—the sound is not so loud that it will prevent you from hearing your cell phone ring.

Television

While American television programs are rebroadcast all around the globe, many foreigners do not realize that these programs are retitled, re-edited and hastily dubbed for the overseas market. You may be shocked to learn Czech is not Remington Steele's first language! Programs you may be familiar with, like "Raymond Loves Everybody," "Richard Dawson's Creek" and "The Chris Kattan Live Saturday Evening Variety Program" exist here in very different forms. Some of the most popular shows in America are:

"SURVIVOR" • In this show's first season, America wondered whether the million dollars would go to the naked mean gay guy or the ancient cracker. The game boiled down to a heated competition over who could hold his hand on a pole longer, which was every bit as exciting as it sounds.

"WILL AND GRACE" • Like "The Ellen Show" and "Frasier," this popular program takes a frank look at the real lives of American homosexuals, minus any sort of obvious affection toward or romantic contact with members of the same sex.

"LAW & ORDER: LAW & ORDER" • Filmed on the set of the hit NBC show "Law & Order," "Law & Order: Law & Order" follows the dedicated men and women who patrol the sets of the police drama "Law & Order" and protect the cast and crew. Sparks fly whenever a groggy Jerry Orbach hollers, "Who do you have to blow around here to get a cup of coffee?"

"IMAGINARY FRIENDS" • At the Central Perk coffeehouse, Joey, Zobert, Shmoo, Xaxxo and Thumbelina hang out and demand salary increases.

CABLE

On cable television, the Discovery Channel broadcasts science and nature shows on a wide variety of subjects, from "Killer Sharks" to "Volcanoes: Are There Sharks in Them?" Award-winning HBO airs shows like "Naked Women," a hard-hitting documentary about women who are, for some reason, naked. MTV's long-running "Real World" series spotlights assholes in different cities around the country.

Radio

Radio survives despite a glut of more interesting media, still offering true dependability and programming variety. Tune in any time of the day, and if you don't hear the same song every time, you'll hear a cover version by another band.

An antidote to noisy, formulaic radio programming is National Public Radio. NPR is where Americans turn for thoughtful commentary presented by sheltered intellectuals in the driest, least entertaining way possible, and for automotive tips.

Books

Reading is a chore for Americans. Most would rather drive off a cliff than read a road sign, so book publishers market to the lowest common denominator. Books for "dummies" and "idiots" sell extremely well, outperforming titles for other kinds of jackasses nearly two to one.

Talk show host Oprah Winfrey single-handedly awakened a huge interest in middlebrow literary fiction with her now-defunct "Oprah's Book Club." Although some booklovers criticized her choices as mediocre and unchallenging, she was lauded by the publishing industry for getting Americans to purchase mediocre, unchallenging books.

Comic Books

Comic books provide young men with a means of escape from their humdrum, non-proton-beam-shooting lives. In America, comic books primarily involve "super-heroes," men and women with incredible, impossible powers like flight, invisibility and the ability to look good in form-fitting clothes. Many famous film and television characters originated in comic books, including Superman, Batman and Charlie Rose.

Sci-Fi

Science-fiction fans in America are divided into two distinct camps: "Star Trek" fans and "Star Wars" fans.

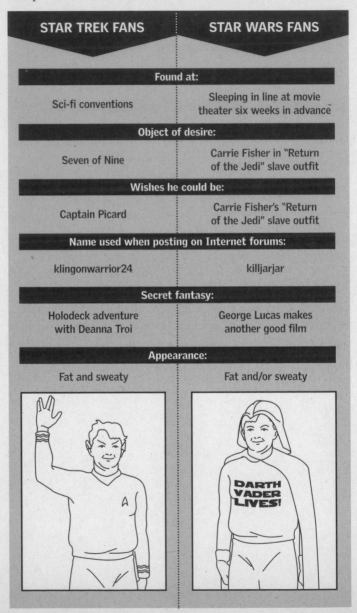

STAR TREK FANS	STAR WARS FANS
Found at:	
Sci-fi conventions	Sleeping in line at movie theater six weeks in advance
Object of desire:	
Seven of Nine	Carrie Fisher in "Return of the Jedi" slave outfit
Wishes he could be:	
Captain Picard	Carrie Fisher's "Return of the Jedi" slave outfit
Name used when posting on Internet forums:	
klingonwarrior24	killjarjar
Secret fantasy:	
Holodeck adventure with Deanna Troi	George Lucas makes another good film
Appearance:	
Fat and sweaty	Fat and/or sweaty

Internet

Entertainment is routinely discussed with great fervor on the Internet. Sci-fi fans and comic book fans and gaming fans and sci-fi gaming fans and comic book gaming fans and sci-fi comic book gaming fans gather in chatrooms and on message boards to debate the finer points of their obsessions and mercilessly "flame" anyone who doesn't speak Klingon or is out of the closet.

Video Games

Many young Americans are mesmerized by video games. But with so many options to choose from, how does one decide?

	MICROSOFT X-BOX	SONY PLAYSTATION 2	MASTURBATION
PROCESSOR	Intel 733MHz processor	128-bit "Emotion Engine"	Parallel-configured 2-ounce testes
PROCESSOR	100 million polygons/second	20 million polygons/second	2 million sperm/second
MEMORY	64 MB	32 MB	20 years
MOST POPULAR GAMES	Halo, Dead or Alive 3, Max Payne	SSX, Tekken Tag Tournament, Madden 2001	Babysitter's Blues, Apprentice Plumber's Pipe, Sexy Secretary's Sick Day
MOST POPULAR CHARACTERS	Taut, buxom, Lara Croft–like heroines	Taut, buxom, Lara Croft–like heroines	Taut, buxom, Lara Croft–like heroines
BENEFITS	Hand-eye coordination	Hand-eye coordination	Hand-penis coordination
HAZARDS	Loss of imagination	Failure to promote actual physical exercise	Both of these, plus blindness

Comedy Clubs

If you enjoy laughter, you might wish to do as Americans do and take a trip to a comedy club. Most every medium-size city has at least one such club, operating under a name like "The Laff Factory," "The Chuckle Hut" or "The Mildly Funny Dwelling." (You may also want to sample some of America's unique brands of local humor, including The Crazy Old Man Down By the Tracks in Sandusky, Illinois, and The Boy Who Can Do That Thing With His Ears in Belmont, New Hampshire.)

Besides the ticket price, there is a two-drink minimum at comedy clubs, meaning you must purchase two alcoholic beverages once inside. This is to ensure that by the time the headlining comedian takes the stage, you are inebriated enough to hoot and laugh maniacally at even the weakest comedy routine, of which there will be four.

Fine Arts

Americans may have a reputation as philistines, but if you visit any art museum in a major city you will find throngs of people inside, enjoying the art and discussing it knowledge-ably. These people are tourists from other countries.

Theater

To many Americans, the word "theater" tends to conjure intimidating images of Greek tragedies or lofty Shakespearean epics. In an attempt to demystify the theater experience for the average citizen, the trend on Broadway has been to base stage shows on popular motion pictures.

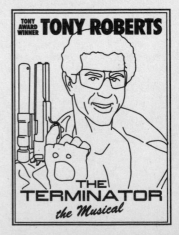

Some theater-goers prefer "edgier" subject matter. They won't be disappointed by shows like "Stomp," about men who bang on garbage cans, "Blue Man Group," about blue men who bang on garbage cans or "The Vagina Monologues," about talking vaginas.

The biggest fallacy about theater in America is that you have to be on Broadway to enjoy it. In fact, theaters have popped up in even the smallest American cities:

America hosts a variety of local theaters

Symphonic Concerts

Classical music is undergoing a resurgence of popularity stateside. First-time concertgoers should know that quiet is appreciated by audience and performers alike. Coughing, talking and any other activity that draws attention away from the concert is cause for angry shushing and speculation about income level.

Not acceptable

Popular Music

Rock and pop music concerts are always well attended in America, which is, after all, the birthplace of rock, blues and the cattle stampede. Be aware that there are countless music subcultures, each with its own fashions and favored intoxicant, and you will feel more comfortable at a concert if you dress and dose accurately.

Goth
(Nine Inch Nails, The Cure)

Rap
(Puff Daddy, Snoop Dogg)

Pop
(Britney Spears, *NSYNC)

Whatever musical group you see, you'll want to visit the merchandise counter to pick up an official logo-imprinted item. Let the world know which pop combo you support!

CHEF'S APRON $40

I'M COOKING WITH ELVIS COSTELLO

CEREAL $4.95

CostellOs
TOASTED OAT CEREAL

$16

$39

I ENJOY THE MUSIC OF ELVIS COSTELLO EVEN THE NEW STUFF

COSTELLO WIPES PAPER TOWELS

BUMPER STICKERS $6

HONK IF YOU LOVE ELVIS COSTELLO

ELVIS COSTELLO FANS MAKE BETTER LOVERS

BUTTONS $3

TAX PREP SOFTWARE $145.99

CostelloQuickTax Prep Software

$25

The typical concert has a well-stocked merchandise counter

Other Musical Genres

Jazz is a purely American musical form that is widely respected but too complicated to be enjoyed by Americans in its undiluted form. Some Americans tolerate "fusion jazz," which takes the random time signatures and melodic inscrutability of pure jazz and "fuses" it with the screaming guitars, volume and silly pomposity of hard rock, rendering it unsatisfying to fans of either genre. Others enjoy "lite jazz," whose most popular exponents are Kenny G and Sting. Lite jazz is very similar to pop music, only with the sad bleat of tenor saxophones added to make the listener feel like a sophisticated jazz lover.

"New Age" music features soothing melodies played on acoustic instruments over whale sounds. If Lite Jazz is the music you hear in your dentist's office, then New Age is the music your dentist hears in his aromatherapist's office and finds too bland. If you go to planetariums or watch documentaries about poor countries for the music, you'll like New Age.

Newspaper Cartoons

American newspapers generally have a page devoted to comic strips, mostly about the work-place, printed at a size where they can be comfortably read with a jeweler's loupe or magnifying glass.

Non-humorous strips also exist—these generally consist of three panels, with one panel advancing the storyline slightly from the previous day.

THE GHOSTLY MAN   **by Gil Seudonimo**

Amusement Parks and Carnivals

America is world-famous for its opulent amusement parks and has even exported Disneyland overseas, so that other cultures may experience the magical fun of a militaristic environment enlivened by cartoon animals. But Americans also enjoy the simple pleasures of the county fair or the arrival of a traveling carnival. These events have rollercoas-ters and ferris wheels that are just like those at large amusement parks but are smaller, more poorly maintained and with less liability insurance.

DATING AND SEX

Though populous, America can be a very lonely place without romantic companionship. There are many ways to find that special someone, whether you're looking for a lifetime relationship or a shameful fifteen-minute encounter.

Mr. Right   **Mr. Right Now**

One common American way to meet people is through "the personals," which are a type of classified advertisement found in free weekly newspapers. In these ads, men and women interested in finding a mate describe themselves in exaggeratedly glowing terms using a variety of baffling acronyms (see sidebar on page 118). Interested readers call a voice mail number and introduce themselves in a similarly misleading manner. Then the two parties meet somewhere they can be reasonably sure they won't see anyone they know, to experience awkward conversation and crushing disappointment.

In larger American cities, it is possible to place a "personal ad" specifically requesting sexual favors. If you are a woman interested in placing such an ad, I would be very surprised.

GLOSSARY OF PERSONAL AD TERMS

Acronyms:

SWF ....Single White Female

SWM ....Single White Male

MWF ....Married White Female

MWM ....Married White Male

MTM..................Mary Tyler Moore

WCW ....World Championship
Wrestling

B...Black

H...Hispanic

A ....Asian

PI............................Pacific Islander,
also Private Investigator

VD....................Vietnamese Descent

GWF ....Grossly Wide Feet

GHM.................Growing Handlebar
Mustache

DJM..............Destructive Japanese
Monster

GJM ....Broadway Actor

TVTS .....Television's Tony Soprano

OTK........Overly Theatrical Karate

OTB ....Off-Track Betting

BDSM.............................Bland Date,
Sexually Meek

No D&D.........No Drugs or Disease

No AD&D....................No Advanced
Dungeons & Dragons

VFAK............Voted for Alan Keyes

RTD&G.................Religiously Tapes
"Dharma and Greg"

SEFH ....Sports Embarrassing
Facial Hair

GSTIC ....Got Stupid Tattoo
in College

TFTLH ....Too Fat to Leave Home

FWHCOSJS..............Former White
House Chief of Staff John Sununu

OTLSFVH.................One-Time Lead
Singer for Van Halen

Phrases:

"comfortable in jeans or a
tuxedo" = I'm a slob, but I
have money

"voluptuous" = fat

"vivacious" = obnoxious

"outgoing" = asshole

"Rubensesque" = fat

"free spirit" = unemployed

"professional" = have had good
jobs in past

"generous men only" = I am
a prostitute

"cuddly teddy bear type" = fat

"Tom Cruise lookalike" = 5'2"

"Earth Mother" = fat

"fit, athletic" = recently lost
four pounds

"spiritual" = flaky

"sensitive" = went off Prozac a
month ago

"has inner beauty" = really,
really fat

DATING AND SEX

Another popular American way for people to meet is by visiting singles bars or dance clubs. Many such clubs, colloquially known as "meet markets," exist almost exclusively to "hook up" lonely singles and sell them six-dollar Long Island iced teas. With their common sense blunted by

The beginning of a lifetime commitment

liquor, the average single American feels more comfortable striking up conversations with total strangers than he or she would if sober. In fact, most relationships in America, from the most casual of encounters to a 45-year marriage, are engendered by an evening of tequila "belly shots."

FUN FACT

DID YOU KNOW...?

American children usually receive an explanation of the "birds and the bees" at age twelve, by which time they've been having unprotected sex for six months.

The preferred American method of making a romantic overture to a patron in a bar is the "pick-up line." This is a question or phrase so clever, flattering or amusing that it will make your quarry mad with sexual desire. Pick-up lines include such witty phrases as "If I said you had a beautiful body, would you hold it against me?" "That's a nice shirt. Can I talk you out of it?" and "I would like to savor the aroma of your genitals." If the kind of contact you are seeking is a hard slap to the face, this technique is infallible.

Note: In some European countries, men commonly pinch the bottoms of strange women. Here in America men look down their shirts instead.

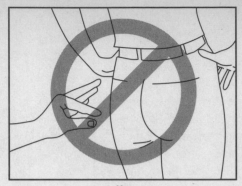

No

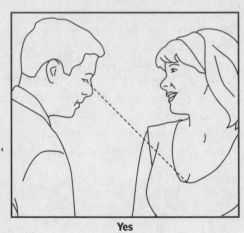

Yes

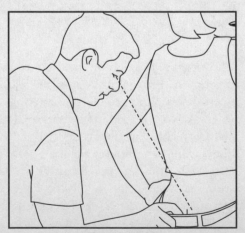

Also acceptable

FUN FACT

DID YOU KNOW...?

In America, the stranger in a bar chatting you up could be female! The Equal Rights movement and the invention of the birth control pill in America in the 1970s made it acceptable for women to initiate romantic and sexual contact with men. Though researchers in the field have yet to encounter such an instance, scientists have replicated it under laboratory conditions.

SUREFIRE PICK-UP LINES

"You look like the best I'll be able to do tonight."

"Can I get you a drink? I mean, you pay for it, but I'll go get it."

"I've been watching you all night, and—oh, wait, it was this other girl who looked like you."

"Was your father a thief? Because I left my jacket by the bar and now my wallet's gone."

"That dress you're wearing would look great on the floor next to my bed. Seriously, the weave matches my duvet cover."

"Gosh, your friend is really pretty. I bet you feel invisible when you're with her, huh?"

"I just made a bet with my friend and we need you to settle it: Are you having your period?"

"I've been working up my courage all night to approach you. There! I did it. Cheers."

Gay/Lesbian

Gay and lesbian communities are slowly becoming more visible in America. Today, in more enlightened cities such as San Francisco and New York City, it is possible to be publicly homosexual and not be chased down the street by pitchfork-carrying locals. (Many states have instituted a pitchfork-purchase waiting period.) Though not universally accepted, gay men and women have made cultural inroads; many of the musical styles, fashions, forms of disrespect and surprised exclamations popular in middle America got their start in the gay community.

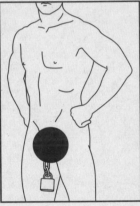

Gay contributions to American culture:
TOP LEFT:
Musical theater
TOP RIGHT:
Penis jewelry
BOTTOM RIGHT:
Bruce Vilanch

Still, only a few cities and neighborhoods are predominantly known for their homosexual population. If you are gay, and want to be near other gay people so as to improve your chances of meeting one, consult this quick reference guide of areas in and around major cities where there is a noted gay population.

> San Francisco: Castro District
> New York City: Greenwich Village
> Boston: Provincetown, a 3-hour drive
> Hawkinsville, Georgia: Provincetown, a 23½-hour drive

Pornography

While Americans can seem embarrassed when confronted with the topic of sex, they privately support the world's largest and most lucrative sex industry. To borrow an American phrase, "Bite it, Sweden!" When it comes to videos, photographs and Web sites depicting sweaty, grinding genitals, America is number one.

One way of relieving the frustration of an empty consumerist life is masturbation. This is frequently aided by pornography. Fortunately, there are several levels of pornography available, depending on your perversion preference.

CHEESECAKE FARE: "Playboy" magazine pioneered the technology of combining political commentary, short stories and hard-hitting interviews with pictures showing underweight, heavily made-up women with large breast implants and intricately sculpted pubic hair. Models tend to be nude but for lingerie or parochial school uniforms.

SOFTCORE: Movies of this sort focus on the female breast, but have a thin semblance of plot. The advantage to softcore pornography is simple: The sex, being more sensual than graphic, is not nearly as offensive to women as some other kinds. Many men feel comfortable watching these films with their wives, yet they are still able to glimpse breasts not belonging to their wives.

HARDCORE: Often used educationally, hardcore videos and magazines show women's internal plumbing.

For more on pornography, visit TeenSlutWarehouse.com.

Strip Clubs

Though Americans are greatly embarrassed by the casual nudity one might face in a locker room or near a breast-feeding mother, they pay large amounts of money to view it in the comfort of a dingy club charging $10 for a plastic cup of ginger ale.

Most strip clubs offer a variety of ways for men to spend their money in exchange for a brief glance of female nudity. First, patrons must pay a hefty "cover charge" to enter the establishment. Once inside, there is generally a large stage area, upon which disinterested young women spastically gyrate to "Welcome to the Jungle." For a fee, you may be able to obtain a "lap dance," which is not as painful as it sounds— the woman does not dance on your lap, but merely sits on top of you for as long as you keep handing over twenty-dollar bills.

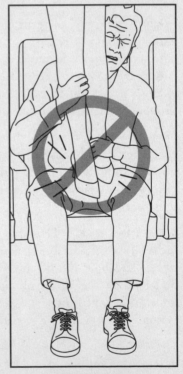

Not a lap dance

Prostitution

No luck finding a date? Not to worry. America is home to a flourishing prostitution trade. Check the local telephone directory and look for "Massage," "Escort Services" or "Nannies." Often, these sorts of businesses are fronts for telemarketers. Read between the lines to discern whether a business is or is not offering sexual favors for money.

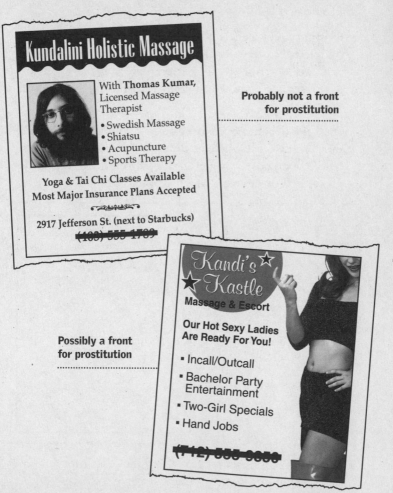

Kundalini Holistic Massage

With **Thomas Kumar,** Licensed Massage Therapist

- Swedish Massage
- Shiatsu
- Acupuncture
- Sports Therapy

Yoga & Tai Chi Classes Available
Most Major Insurance Plans Accepted

2917 Jefferson St. (next to Starbucks)
~~(100) 555 1709~~

Probably not a front for prostitution

Kandi's Kastle
Massage & Escort

Our Hot Sexy Ladies Are Ready For You!

- Incall/Outcall
- Bachelor Party Entertainment
- Two-Girl Specials
- Hand Jobs

~~(712) 555 8858~~

Possibly a front for prostitution

Prostitution Etiquette

In America, as in your own country, there are unspoken rules for soliciting and employing a professional sex worker. Even those of you for whom such things are "old hat" and as natural as eating Gouda cheese in a field of windmills should realize that it's different in America. To avoid embarrassing incidents, keep in mind the following guidelines:

- Prostitution is illegal in America except in one state and on television networks like Fox and MTV. Streetwalkers will not describe their services for fear that you are a policeman; you must ask verbally for what you want orally.

- Once the deal has been struck, relax. You're in the hands of a professional who has done this thousands of times before, perhaps even seven times today, on the same grotty bed or table on which you're lying.

- Don't relax too much. There have been reported cases of sex workers stealing more than just bodily fluids.

- When everything is over, thank your prostitute politely and give him or her a good tip. If you were disappointed in the service or discovered that the prostitute was not the gender you had hoped for, leave a smaller tip.

CLOTHING

Perhaps you've seen Americans visiting your home country. They are easy to spot, as they very much resemble billboards. Often wide and plastered with logos, Americans enjoy being free advertising for faceless corporate masters, and paying top dollar for the privilege. Note these examples of advertising on clothing.

Statement of support for arena-rock band

Statement of support for hard liquor

Statement of support for the World Wildlife Fund and the critically endangered Sumatran rabbit

In America, caste is not easily determined by clothing. Is that lip-pierced woman with dreadlocks, dirty leather jacket and Misfits T-shirt a street person or a college student? Is the twenty-something man in the Exxon jacket a gas station employee or a record store clerk? Is the suave gentleman in the three-piece suit an executive, or a cocaine-crazed axe murderer who keeps the severed limbs of his victims in a climate-controlled box hidden under the floorboards of his pricey SoHo loft?

These are extreme examples. The great majority of Americans tend to favor loose-fitting casual clothing such as T-shirts and sweatpants. This, of course, is because they are monstrously obese.

FUN FACT

DID YOU KNOW...?

The average American owns 17,568 T-shirts.

Fashion Industry

The American fashion industry is a vibrant field full of opportunity for both gay men and balding gay men. As any fashion television program will make you keenly aware, the purpose of fashion is twofold: To make sure that ugly rock musicians have wives and to make sure the populace never forgets the song "Obsession" by Animotion. The focus of fashion changes on a whim, often from sickly-looking young women with anorexia to the considerably healthier looking bulimics. Those who wish to become models are advised to be born Dutch.

FUN FACT

DID YOU KNOW...?

Denim "blue jeans," now a worldwide fashion staple, originated in America when cowboys working on the range found that the tough, durable pants made their asses look great.

American Hairstyles

As the face of America evolves, so does its hairstyle. You'll note that hairstyles are often named for people who made them popular:

❶ The "Clooney," named for actor George Clooney

❷ The "Rachel," named for the character played by actress Jennifer Aniston

❸ The "Flattop," named for notorious criminal Flattop

SHOPPING

The easy availability of credit cards with usurious interest rates means that American citizens have a virtually unlimited amount of borrowed money with which to shop for goods and services. Shopping is arguably the most popular American activity (rivaled only by eating and talking on the phone about television), and one of the easiest for foreigners to enjoy, as it resembles shopping in other lands.

Malls

The center of American spending is the shopping mall. (For more about America's largest mall, see page 32). Much like the "town square" of 19th-century America, the shopping mall has become a focal point for social activities, including concerts,

Mockery of thieves

holiday celebrations and the mockery of thieves.

Malls are usually equipped with a centrally located court-yard surrounded by fast-food restaurants, colloquially called a "food court." Here you can sample the cuisines of many lands, as interpreted by the food-service branches of giant American conglomerates.

A typical food court

Outlet Malls

Outlet malls are justifiably famous for their adverse environmental impact on what were once wetlands and prairie ecosystems, but did you know that they also sell name-brand American goods at great low prices? The shops in these malls stock discontinued or irregular items, so if your fashion sense or body type leans toward the discontinued or irregular, you'll want to shop here.

High-End vs. Low-End Stores

There are a wide variety of American shops to accommodate the vast range of American interests and incomes, from the tony boutiques of Beverly Hills to the street vendors of midtown Manhattan.

High-end shopping   Low-end shopping

Low-end or "discount" stores are usually recognizable by signage offering improbably discounted merchandise, such as "Now in Our 40th Year of Going Out of Business! Sale on Brand Names: Ray-Band, Clavin Kline, Roalex and Tampax watches!"

Coupons

To employ this money-saving tactic, one need only purchase a magazine or Sunday newspaper, carefully clip the coupon along its dashed border, drive to a store that accepts coupons, find the exact product mentioned in the coupon, bring it to the checkout area, wait in line, present the item and the coupon, and voilà! You've just saved ten cents! Too much work? Well, if that's the way you feel, you go ahead and piss away that dime, Mister Rockefeller.

FUN FACT

DID YOU KNOW...?

An American size 10 dress corresponds to a European size 38. You can easily convert American sizes to European by applying the same formula that you use to convert Fahrenheit temperatures to Centigrade ($Tc = (5/9) \times (Tf-32)$). And you can easily convert your European or other foreign size to an American one by consuming twice your weight in butter every day.

New Chain Stores Coming Soon

NIKE 'N' MORE: Only products that sports superstar Michael Jordan has endorsed are sold here. Be like Mike and get Hanes underwear, Oakley sunglasses, Coach Leather products and much more while snacking on Ballpark Franks and Wheaties.

PIPE ORGANS FOR LESS: Name-brand pipe organs (Tellers, Casavant, Kilgen, Moller, Estey, and others) at great prices. If you play the pipe organ or just like to have one in the house, make a stop here.

ARGON 'N' THINGS: This store stocks all the noble gases and even a few of the halogens.

THE GREAT AMERICAN PUSSY COMPANY: Books, calendars, plush toys and silly gifts for the vagina-lover.

RECREATION

Sports

Americans love sports. Watching them, that is, not playing them. Americans feel a special loyalty to their area's sports teams, who are usually named for a unique local animal or feature. For instance, basketball's Utah Jazz pay tribute to the state's rich musical heritage.

Besides the visceral thrills they provide, competitive sports have become an ice-breaker between American males. An American man would never attempt to strike up a conversation with a male stranger by commenting about music or art, for fear that those comments would be interpreted as a sexual overture. Conversely, if one limits his remarks to sports banter, he need not be worried about accusations of liking culture or men.

"Hey, how about those Dodgers?"

Yes

"I enjoy the bold colors employed in the works of Henri Matisse."

No

TYPES OF
AMERICAN SPORTS

Baseball

Baseball is referred to as America's favorite pastime after Internet pornography. Baseball is not as popular outside America, so you may find the rules hard to understand and the action hard to follow. But you'll find the competition among spec-

tators for balls hit into the stands resembles the soccer riots you're accustomed to.

Basketball

Basketball is an intensely strategic game: Should I sign with Nike or with Reebok? Should I try to parlay my success on the court into a film career or marry Carmen Electra? Should I throw a chair at my coach or choke him? The players who make the right moves on and off the court gain enormous power, wealth, fame and the respect of Woody Allen.

Football (American)

Distantly related to rugby, soccer and aggravated assault, football is followed religiously by American men. Some sociologists think that its popularity stems from its military jargon and controlled violence, which give American men a safe outlet for war fantasies, while others believe that the structure of the game—a few seconds of chaotic action followed by long periods of awkward inactivity—reminds men of sex.

Soccer

Soccer is what you call "football," and what Americans call "fucking lame."

Hockey

This Canadian sport is gradually becoming an American favorite due to the violent, mouth-smashing brawls that take place between parents of adolescent players.

Golf

Once thought of as a boring "old man's sport," golf has become increasingly popular among thrill-seeking young Americans, thanks to its association with adequate rock combo Hootie and the Blowfish.

Wrestling

With its predominance of oiled, semi-nude musclemen with names like "The Rock" and "Mr. Ass," American pro wrestling is intended to inspire and recruit gay children.

TIPS FOR SPECTATORS

Cheering

While viewing a live sporting event many fans attempt to help the home team win the game by offering helpful advice and constructive profanity. This is called "cheering," and American sporting fans typically relish the moment to make their opinions heard.

To assist you in making your own cheers while you attend a game, try clipping out this handy chart:

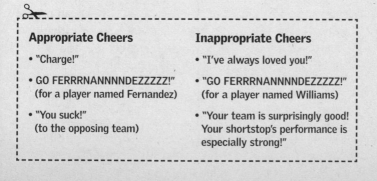

Appropriate Cheers	Inappropriate Cheers
• "Charge!"	• "I've always loved you!"
• GO FERRRNANNNNDEZZZZZ!" (for a player named Fernandez)	• "GO FERRRNANNNNDEZZZZZ!" (for a player named Williams)
• "You suck!" (to the opposing team)	• "Your team is surprisingly good! Your shortstop's performance is especially strong!"

Tickets

Be sure you are purchasing your tickets from a licensed ticket vendor, as "scalpers" may attempt to sell you counterfeit tickets for far more than the official purchase price. The term "scalper" originated in America's colonial period, when marauding bands of unlicensed vendors sold tickets to "The Producers."

Licensed vendor

Unlicensed vendor

Unlicensed Vader

Dress

Eager to participate in the games without actually having to play them, American spectators often wear outlandish costumes and engage in wild antics in order to boost their team's morale and get themselves on television.

Typical American sports fans

"Extreme" Sports

Teenage Americans have become quite interested in outdoor sports in recent years, especially so-called extreme sports. Youngsters enjoy the endorphin rush of these "edgy," "alternative," and "spine-damaging" stunts.

Part of the appeal of "extreme" sports is their outlaw, "break all the rules" attitude. So if you participate in extreme sports, try to break every rule that you can, whether it's "Wear protective gear," "Not for pregnant women" or "Write account number on face of check."

Snowboarding

Headbanging

**Running on Fumes
(a.k.a. Jumping the Shark)**

Hunting and Fishing

Contrary to popular belief, not all hunters are redneck, Schlitz-swilling, gun-toting yahoos. Many use crossbows instead. In America, hunting is not only a means of finding food, but also a perfectly legal sublimation of the instinctual desire to find, track, shoot, and gut another human being. Plus, it offers an opportunity to wear bright orange without being mocked.

For those who consider beer and boats a safer combination than beer and guns, fishing is also popular. Sometimes called "fishin'," this pastime takes the ordinarily dull activity of doing nothing and livens it up with the addition of drifting.

Wildlife

If you encounter a bear unexpectedly, he may be startled enough to attack. Make noise while hiking through wilderness areas so that bears hear you coming. Clap your hands, talk loudly or carry a noise-making device.

Hike safely

Bears may also be attracted to your campsite by the smell of food. Should you see a hungry bear approach your camp-ground, it's a good idea to feed it appetite suppressant tablets such as Dexatrim—the bear will feel full, albeit very jittery and self-conscious.

FINAL WORDS

Is This a Great F***ing Country Or What?

Congratulations! You are now ready to visit America. Culturally aware and armed to the teeth, you can walk among its citizenry without fear of embarrassment or bludgeoning. Unfortunately, there is not enough space in one volume to describe all that America has to offer: In subsequent volumes, we will examine go-kart racing, the city of Fresno, California, and the heartbreaking plight of the American Indian. There's so much to enjoy in America, you may never want to leave!

By the time you finish reading this page, 3,000 Americans will take a bullet, 3 million will super-size their Happy Meals and three will pass a geography test. Still, this nation is the envy of the world, except in Sweden, where government subsidies ensure all citizens have equal access to health care and erotica.

Remember that America is a Land of Opportunity, the place where your dreams come true, whether you want to become a pop superstar, make millions by defrauding stockholders, or marry a rich weirdo on television. Opportunity is the beauty of this land. That, and the purple mountain majesties, the fruited plain and the comforting fact that there's an Abercrombie & Fitch within three miles of where you're sitting.

Happy trails, and enjoy your visit to the bestest country ever!